LEADING BY SERVING

Leading by Serving

Fundamentals of Servant Leadership

THOMAS A MAYBERRY

Copyright © 2024 by Thomas Mayberry

All rights reserved. No part of this book may be reproduced in any manner whatsoever without written permission except in the case of brief quotations embodied in critical articles and reviews.

First Printing, 2024

Whatever you do, work at it with all your heart, as working for the Lord, not for human masters, since you know that you will receive an inheritance from the Lord as a reward. It is the Lord Christ you are serving.
Colossians 3:23-24 (NIV)

Do you have the gift of speaking? Then speak as though God himself were speaking through you. Do you have the gift of helping others? Do it with all the strength and energy that God supplies. Then everything you do will bring glory to God through Jesus Christ. All glory and power to him forever and ever! Amen.
1 Peter 4:11 (NLT)

I thank God for the parents He blessed me with, who instilled in me the value and power of the Christian faith. May everything I do bring you glory, and let your light shine through me and my actions so others can get to know you.

Contents

Dedication		v
Acknowledgement		ix
Preface		xi
1	The Two Types of Leaders	1
2	The Power of Empathy	9
3	Leading by Example	15
4	Nurturing Growth and Development	29
5	The Upside Down Organizational Chart	39
6	Cultivating Collaboration	45
7	Developing your Team Members	51
8	The Ripple Effect of Servant Leadership	55
9	Self-evaluation	65
10	Transformational vs Servant Leadership	71
11	Jesus as the Ultimate Servant Leader	79
12	Why be a Servant?	89
About The Author		95

Acknowledgement

I want to give a special thank you to Martha Rushing for her incredible patience as I continue to bounce ideas off of her and consult with her in editing my files. As I was coming to the end of the process of this book, I was struggling to come up with ideas about the design of the cover. She helped guide me in the right direction, and I am so pleased with the outcome. I cannot thank you enough for all you do for me.

Preface

Imagine changing your leadership approach and witnessing a remarkable, far-reaching shift in both your professional career and personal life. This experience is precisely what I underwent, and I'm thoroughly convinced that you can achieve similar life-altering results. The power of adopting a new leadership mindset extends far beyond the confines of the workplace. By embracing change and cultivating a more effective leadership style, you open doors to unprecedented opportunities and personal development, creating a ripple effect that touches not only your own life but also the lives of those around you.

Let me take you on a journey through my personal experience, spanning decades, and offers valuable insights into the complexities of ambition and its consequences. In the early 1980s, I emerged from college as a fresh graduate, armed with a management degree and brimming with enthusiasm for the future. My mind was filled with dreams of success and a burning desire to prove myself professionally.

At that time, I was driven by two primary forces: an intense ambition to climb the corporate ladder and a fierce competitive spirit that pushed me to outperform my peers. These traits, which I initially perceived as assets, seemed to align perfectly with the cutthroat business environment of the era. I threw myself into my career with unwavering determination, working long hours and constantly seeking advancement opportunities. However, as the years progressed, I realized that these qualities that propelled my professional success were taking a heavy toll on my personal life. The relentless pursuit of career goals left little time or energy for nurturing relationships, particularly my marriage.

My passion for leadership was undeniable. I devoured leadership books and aspired to be a keynote speaker. I even started compiling traits of great leaders, not realizing I was laying the groundwork for my future book. However, I lost sight of my true beliefs, emulating the cutthroat leadership styles around me.

It wasn't until I reached my mid-30s that I experienced a profound and pivotal realization: I needed to realign my life with my core values. This introspective journey led me to embrace the philosophy of servant leadership. This approach, which prioritizes the growth and well-being of others, resonated deeply with my innate beliefs and aspirations.

As I began implementing servant leadership principles in my personal and professional life, I noticed a remarkable change. Suddenly, everything seemed to fall into place with an almost effortless synchronicity. My relationships improved, my sense of purpose deepened, and I found a renewed sense of fulfillment in my daily activities. Perhaps most surprisingly, success began to follow naturally due to this shift in perspective. Focusing on serving others and contributing to the greater good, I discovered that personal and professional achievements came more easily and felt more meaningful.

As I reconnected with my Christian faith, I discovered that the leadership traits I admired were deeply rooted in biblical principles. This revelation led to my first book, *Faith Guided Leadership*, in 2011. My mission became clear: to guide others away from the pitfalls I encountered early in my career.

Delving deeper into servant leadership, I found a profound truth: when you prioritize others' success, your own career flourishes. It's a beautiful cycle of mutual growth and achievement.

Now, I invite you to embark on your own leadership transformation. Use this book as a mirror to reflect on your leadership style. Identify your strengths and areas for improvement. By applying these principles and nurturing others' potential, I guarantee you'll see a significant positive change in your life.

True leadership isn't about personal gain but elevating those around you. Are you ready to revolutionize your approach and reap the rewards of servant leadership? The choice is yours, and the growth potential is limitless.

Chapter 1

The Two Types of Leaders

Leader First vs. Servant First

The concept of servant leadership has existed for over 2000 years. Jesus not only taught the concept, but He lived it every day. He may not have used that specific term, but it describes His approach to all aspects of His life here on Earth. In Mark 10:45, Jesus says it was His whole reason for being here. "For even the Son of Man did not come to be served, but to serve, and to give His life as a ransom for many." This powerful statement serves as the cornerstone for servant leadership. It teaches us that authentic leadership is not about getting people to serve you but selflessly serving others. Even the ultimate Leader, Jesus, came to serve, setting an excellent example for us.

It was not until 1970 that Robert K. Greenleaf coined the term in his influential essay "The Servant as Leader." The idea of the servant as leader came from his encounter with the character Leo in Hermann Hesse's Journey to the East.

This story shows a band of men on a mythical journey...The story's central figure is Leo, who accompanies the party as the servant who does their menial chores and sustains them with his spirit and song. He is a person of extraordinary presence. All goes well until Leo disappears. Then, the group falls into disarray, and the journey is abandoned. They cannot make it without the servant Leo. After some years of wandering, the narrator, one of the party, finds Leo and is taken into the Order that had sponsored the journey. There, he discovers that Leo, whom he had known first as a servant, was, in fact, the titular head of the Order, its guiding spirit, a great and noble leader.[i] Struck by Leo's role as a servant whose absence led to a decline in productivity among other workers, Greenleaf was inspired to explore the notion that authentic leadership could emerge from a position of service rather than authority.

Greenleaf's encounter with Leo inspired him to champion servant leadership, a model that fosters trust and autonomy between leaders and their teams. He put this theory to the test during his tenure at AT&T, where he witnessed its power in fostering a culture of collaboration and empowerment. Greenleaf's belief in humility, empathy, and service deeply influenced his perspective on leadership. He saw servant leadership as a practical way to apply these spiritual principles in the context of organizations and society, a belief that was reinforced by his experiences at AT&T.

While Greenleaf's concept of servant leadership is not explicitly tied to any specific religious tradition, its roots in his Christian faith are evident in his writings and speeches. He often referenced religious texts and figures, such as Jesus' teachings on servant leadership, as inspiration for his ideas. In his 1970 book, The Servant as a Leader, He refers to the concept of the servant-leader as akin to the idea of a servant of God, highlighting the moral and ethical dimensions of leadership.

"Good leaders must first become good servants."
Robert Greenleaf

Central to Greenleaf's concept of servant leadership are two fundamental premises: "I serve because I am the leader" and "I am the leader because I serve." The former underscores the importance of altruism and selflessness in leadership, emphasizing a leader's commitment to serving the needs of others. The latter premise highlights the reciprocal relationship between serving and leading, suggesting that authentic leadership emerges from a genuine desire to serve others rather than a quest for personal ambition.

Over the years, Greenleaf's ideas have gained traction as an effective leadership style, resonating with leaders across various industries who seek to cultivate trust, inspire collaboration, and empower their teams to achieve collective success. Through the lens of servant leadership, leaders are encouraged to prioritize the well-being and growth of their team members, recognizing that authentic leadership lies in service to others.

Robert K. Greenleaf distinguished between two different types of leaders: servant-first and leader-first.

- A leader-first leader will likely focus on being direct and achieving personal and professional goals. Their primary focus will be growing their career through their team's performance and output. They have an "It's all about me" attitude.

- A servant-first leader surrenders most of their authority and prioritizes their team. This selfless type of leadership focuses on team members' well-being and long-term growth.

Although "leader" and "servant" may seem paradoxical, leaders who serve their team by encouraging growth, offering a sense of purpose, and presenting a clear vision create an environment where team members feel welcomed and supported.

I have worked for leader-first leaders. They are the first to take credit for what their teams have accomplished while showing little acknowledgment of the individual successes of the team members. They blame those reporting to them if a project does not meet all the goals. They do not "own" responsibility for falling short. Leader-first leaders have a huge ego and desire to continue feeding it. They must have a title that demands respect from their team. The leader believes they always have the correct answers to improve the operation. They would not think of soliciting ideas from the team, and if a good idea comes up, they will somehow spin it to where it comes across as their idea so they can take the credit.

Another way of looking at this type of leader is they are self-serving leaders. They worry about keeping their status and respond negatively to feedback. They are addicted to power and recognition and do not spend much time training their replacement because it may mean they would lose their position.

Then, there is the servant leader. They put others' needs and well-being above their own. At the beginning of His ministry, we see Jesus preparing to lead by His acts of submission and testing of His character.

In Matthew 3:13-17 (NKJV) we read

Then Jesus came from Galilee to John at the Jordan to be baptized by him. And John tried to prevent Him, saying "I need to be baptized by You, and You are coming to me?" But Jesus answered and said to him, "Permit it to be so now, for thus it is fitting for us to fulfill all righteousness." Then he allowed Him. When He had been baptized, Jesus came up immediately from the water; and behold, the heavens were open to Him, and He saw the Spirit of God descending like a dove and alighting upon Him. And suddenly a voice came from heaven saying, "This is My beloved Son, in whom I am well pleased."

In His interaction with John, Jesus demonstrated two very significant attributes of servant leadership. He validated and affirmed John in his ministry and submitted Himself to the same acts of surrender to doing what He would require of others. A servant leader never asks anyone to do something they are unwilling to do themselves.[ii]

Maybe you haven't thought much about servant leadership and are still new to the concept. Take a moment to reflect on the individuals who have left a lasting impression on you throughout your professional journey. Remember those mentors, colleagues, and leaders who inspired you and made a difference in your life. What characteristics did they display that impressed you the most? How did their presence and actions regularly make the people around them feel?

As we delve deeper into the traits of a servant-first leader, you'll likely recognize these qualities in those remarkable individuals who have touched your life. Their impact wasn't just about their accomplishments but about how they lifted others up and created an environment of growth and empowerment. Now, let's turn the spotlight inward. What defines your style of leadership? What traits do you exhibit in your interactions with others? Are you fostering collaboration and mutual respect, or is there room for improvement? It's crucial to ask yourself these questions with honesty and openness.

Does your pride sometimes act as a barrier, preventing you from growing as a leader? It's human nature to find it challenging to admit our faults, but this very act of vulnerability is how we grow and evolve. Remember, none of us has all the answers or never makes mistakes. Sometimes, we all fall short of expectations and goals – it's part of the human experience and the leadership journey. The leader-first approach often emphasizes where an idea originates rather than the merit of the idea itself. This mindset can stifle creativity and collaboration. We must turn that philosophy around and embrace a more inclusive, servant-first approach. Imagine the possibilities when we focus on nurturing ideas and supporting our team members, regardless of their position or status. As you continue on your leadership journey, challenge yourself to cultivate the traits of a servant leader. Embrace humility, prioritize the growth of others, and create an environment where everyone feels valued and heard. By doing so, you'll become a more effective leader and inspire those around you to reach their full potential. Remember, true leadership isn't about being in charge; it's about caring for those in your charge.

In a world that often glorifies power-driven leadership styles, embracing the essence of servant leadership can be truly transformative. It reminds us that true strength lies in our ability to uplift others and make a positive impact through our actions. As followers of Jesus, we already know this approach works. He was the ultimate example of being a servant leader. In Mark 10:42-45 (NIV) we read *Jesus called them together and said, "You know that those who are regarded as rulers of the Gentiles lord it over them, and their high officials exercise authority over them. Not so with you. Instead, whoever wants to become great among you must be your servant, and whoever wants to be first must be slave of all. For even the Son of Man did not come to be served, but to serve, and to give his life as a ransom for many."* Even with His power to rule the world, He did not come to us to be served but to serve. Look how many followers He has added to His flock over the years with this approach. We do not look at Jesus as being a lesser being because of being a servant.

In our fast-paced, achievement-driven culture, we often overlook the true value of those who dedicate their lives to serving others. Sadly, we witness countless instances where hardworking individuals in the service industry are treated with disdain or indifference, their contributions diminished by the very people they strive to assist. This misguided attitude stems from a flawed perception that places some on a pedestal while relegating others to a subservient role, creating an unhealthy imbalance in human interactions. It's time for a profound shift in our collective mindset. We must recognize that serving others is not a burden thrust upon us, but a precious opportunity to make a meaningful difference in someone's life.

Each act of service, no matter how small, has the power to create ripples of positivity that extend far beyond the immediate interaction. When we embrace this perspective, we unlock the transformative potential of compassion and empathy. Let us aspire to cultivate a society where service is revered as a noble calling, where those who dedicate themselves to the well-being of others are celebrated and respected. By reframing our understanding of service as a privilege rather than an obligation, we open our hearts to the joy of giving and the profound satisfaction of uplifting our fellow human beings. Together, we can create a world where kindness and mutual respect flourish, inspiring generations to come.

Chapter 2

The Power of Empathy

Building strong connections with your team

A Servant leader embodies a unique blend of qualities that set them apart in their approach to leadership. At the core of their philosophy lies empathy and humility, two essential virtues that serve as the foundation for building solid and meaningful relationships with their team members.

Empathy, the ability to understand and share the feelings of others, allows servant leaders to connect with their team on a profound level. By actively listening and showing genuine concern for their colleagues' thoughts, feelings, and experiences, they cultivate an environment of trust and openness. This empathy enables them to perceive each team member's needs and aspirations, recognizing that everyone brings unique talents, challenges, and ambitions.

It can be as said as in Romans 12:15, *"Rejoice with those who rejoice, weep with those who weep."* Celebrate with them as they celebrate the essential parts of their lives and feel their pain when they suffer. Another way to say it is in 1 Corinthians 12:26. *"If one member suffers, all suffer together; if one member is honored, all rejoice together."*

Empathy allows you to put yourself in someone else's shoes, enabling you to make informed decisions considering the needs and feelings of those around you. It helps you build rapport with your team members by showing them that you genuinely care about their success and personal growth. Remember, empathy is not just a soft skill but a powerful tool that can transform your leadership style and positively impact your team's performance. Leading with empathy inspires loyalty, motivation, and creativity among your team members. You can create an inclusive workplace where everyone thrives personally and professionally.

We can learn a valuable lesson from Jesus about empathy. Jesus came to earth to live as God in human skin. He suffered the same way we suffer. He experienced pain as we do, but in some cases, at a much higher level. Jesus suffered physically. He was pursued by crowds when trying to be alone, and He was stripped, beaten, spit on, and even made to carry the cross used to crucify Him. He suffered emotionally. He was misunderstood, criticized, mocked, and belittled. He was constantly questioned and challenged, betrayed, and ultimately sentenced to death even though He was innocent. Jesus also suffered relationally. He was unwelcome, heaped with unfair expectations, mislabeled, underestimated, gossiped about, plotted against, and abandoned. He endured all of this for us! I am still in awe of the amount of love He has for us.

Matthew tells the story of the feeding of the five thousand in Matthew 14:13-21 (NIV)

LEADING BY SERVING ~ 11

When Jesus heard what had happened, he withdrew by boat privately to a solitary place. Hearing of this, the crowds followed him on foot from the towns. When Jesus landed and saw a large crowd, he had compassion on them and healed their sick. As evening approached, the disciples came to him and said, "This is a remote place, and it's already getting late. Send the crowds away, so they can go to the villages and buy themselves some food." Jesus replied, "They do not need to go away. You give them something to eat." "We have here only five loaves of bread and two fish," they answered. "Bring them here to me," he said. And he directed the people to sit down on the grass. Taking the five loaves and the two fish and looking up to heaven, he gave thanks and broke the loaves. Then he gave them to the disciples, and the disciples gave them to the people. They all ate and were satisfied, and the disciples picked up twelve basketfuls of broken pieces that were left over. The number of those who ate was about five thousand men, besides women and children.[iii]

Jesus' ministry was marked by acts of compassion and empathy towards those suffering, demonstrating his deep commitment to serving the needs of others, particularly the marginalized and oppressed. Throughout his ministry, Jesus performed numerous healing miracles, restoring sight to the blind, hearing to the deaf, mobility to the paralyzed, and health to the sick. These miraculous acts were not merely displays of power but manifestations of Jesus' servant leadership and profound compassion for those in need.

He can empathize with us when we suffer. He has experienced the same feelings. If you are suffering today, you are not alone. Jesus is by your side. We need to take this same approach with our team. Empathize with what they are experiencing. You have probably been in that same situation at some point. If not, talk with them to understand what they are going through.

Earlier in my career, I was managing a full-service restaurant. It was a busy Friday night, and I worked in the kitchen. Because of budget cutbacks, the general manager had the evening off. There were only two managers in the restaurant that evening. The only way we got a day off was for the other manager to work a double shift. This was my double shift. I had a shift leader working in the dining room that evening. The kitchen staff was falling behind on the orders. I decided to jump in on the line and assist the cooks.

Because of my frustration, I got in too big of a hurry. When trying to blacken a steak, I threw the steak into the pan, and the grease flew back into my face. I told the staff to call and inform the general manager of the situation. He would need to cover for me while I went to the hospital. I had second-degree burns on my face. I came back to the restaurant after a couple of hours. The general manager greeted me. He did not ask me how I was doing. He told me he had brought me a clean white shirt and tie so I could finish the shift, and he was going home. How was that for compassion? It is not the first step towards being empathetic.

Do we go the extra mile for this person? I would not. I would tend to do just enough, do my own thing, and stay out of the way. I was not about to go the extra mile to make them look better. On the other hand, I have had managers who truly cared about my well-being, and I would go to war with them. I would dig in and help the team rise above the pack. Isn't this what you would like to accomplish? You do not have to get intimately involved in every aspect of their lives, but listening to their concerns and struggles can go a long way.

Coupled with empathy, humility guides the servant leader to approach their role with modesty and self-awareness. They understand that leadership is not about wielding power or seeking personal glory but about serving the greater good and uplifting those around them. With humility as their compass, inspirational leaders readily acknowledge their own limitations, viewing them not as weaknesses but as opportunities for growth and connection. They recognize the immense value in the diverse talents, experiences, and perspectives of their team members, creating an environment where every voice is heard and every contribution is celebrated.

This humble approach nurtures a vibrant culture of collaboration, where mutual respect flourishes and collective wisdom prevails. In embracing humility, servant leaders become beacons of inspiration, demonstrating that true strength lies not in domination but in the ability to uplift others. They show us that by setting aside ego and embracing a spirit of service, we can create workplaces and communities where everyone feels valued, empowered, and inspired to reach their fullest potential. Through their example, these leaders remind us that the most profound impact often comes from those who lead from a humble heart and a steadfast commitment to the well-being of others.

With empathy and humility as guiding principles, servant leaders prioritize the growth and well-being of their team members above all else. Rather than focusing solely on their success or advancing their agendas, they invest time and energy into supporting the development and fulfillment of those they lead. They provide mentorship, guidance, and resources to empower individuals to reach their full potential, recognizing that the team's success is intricately tied to the growth and success of each member.

At its core, being a servant leader means putting others first and being there for your team genuinely and caring. It's all about getting where your team comes from and what they want to achieve. By making empathy and humility a big deal, servant leaders set the stage for trust to grow, teamwork to shine, and everyone to reach their full potential together.

Creating a caring work environment starts with active listening and open communication. By encouraging open dialogue and creating a safe space for sharing ideas or concerns, you empower your team members to express themselves authentically. This cultivates a sense of belonging where everyone feels respected and valued.

Servant leadership boils down to being super committed to serving your team. A natural servant leader always seeks chances to back up and lift their team members. They create a vibe where everyone feels free to speak up, work together, and rely on each other. By embracing this leadership style, organizations can experience profound benefits. Servant leaders create a culture where individuals feel valued and motivated to contribute their best efforts. Team collaboration flourishes under the guidance of a servant leader.

Chapter 3

Leading by Example

Inspiring Trust and Accountability

Leading by example is a powerful management strategy beyond mere role modeling. It initiates a cascading effect of trust and accountability throughout an organization or team. When leaders consistently demonstrate integrity, transparency, and ethical behavior, they establish a clear operational standard without requiring explicit instructions.

This approach creates a tangible blueprint for employees to follow. As leaders exhibit desirable behaviors such as putting in extra effort, admitting mistakes, or offering assistance, it motivates team members to elevate their performance. The willingness of these leaders to invest themselves fully in their work speaks volumes about their dedication. It's not merely about completing tasks; it's about infusing each action with purpose and passion. This level of commitment doesn't go unnoticed; rather, it subtly ignites a similar drive within team members. The effect is akin to positive contagion within the workplace.

> "Servant leadership is all about making the goals clear and then rolling your sleeves up and doing whatever it takes to help people win. In that situation, they don't work for you; you work for them." Kenneth H. Blanchard

Leading by example creates a powerful form of positive peer influence within organizations. This approach encourages individuals to elevate their standards, not because of formal rules or policies, but because of the organizational culture it cultivates. When leaders consistently demonstrate exemplary behavior, it establishes a workplace environment where accountability and ethical conduct become integral parts of the company's ethos. This method effectively promotes an automated system where employees naturally align their actions with the high standards set by their leaders, fostering a more responsible and ethical workplace overall.

Leading by example effectively cultivates a positive organizational culture, promotes accountability, and enhances overall performance without relying on rigid rules or directives. Servant leadership is characterized by a leader's commitment to walking alongside their team members, guiding them through their journey, and leading by example every step. This approach fosters a strong sense of camaraderie and mutual respect within the team, as members witness firsthand their manager's dedication and integrity. When team members observe their leaders willingly investing the same time, effort, and commitment into projects as they do, it cultivates a deep sense of appreciation and admiration. This recognition of their manager's willingness to roll up their sleeves and dive into the trenches alongside them inspires team members to approach their work with renewed vigor and dedication. They feel valued and supported, knowing their leader is fully committed to the team's success.

Servant leaders who lead by example in their dedication to work and commitment to self-care foster a positive and supportive team culture. Embodying integrity, dedication, and genuine concern for their team's well-being, they inspire members to work hard, prioritize self-care, and achieve success together. Integrity forms the backbone of leading by example. Leaders who uphold their values and principles, even when faced with difficult decisions or tempting shortcuts, earn their team's trust and respect.

By consistently acting in alignment with their words and beliefs, they build a reputation for reliability and honesty, inspiring confidence in their leadership. This integrity extends to how servant leaders approach their work responsibilities. They consistently demonstrate a strong work ethic, meeting deadlines, maintaining high standards, and going above and beyond when necessary. This dedication sets a clear expectation for team members and motivates them to match this level of commitment.

However, servant leaders also recognize the importance of balance and self-care. They model healthy work-life boundaries, take time for personal wellness, and encourage their team to do the same. This approach prevents burnout and fosters long-term sustainability within the team. By openly discussing their self-care practices and supporting team members in their personal well-being efforts, these leaders create an environment where individuals feel valued as whole persons, not just as workers. This holistic approach to leadership often results in increased job satisfaction, improved mental health, and enhanced overall team performance.

> *"In everything set them an example by doing what is good. In your teaching show integrity, seriousness and soundness of speech that cannot be condemned, so that those who oppose you may be ashamed because they have nothing bad to say about us."* Titus 2:7-8 (NIV)

Transparency is another critical component. Leaders who are open and honest about their actions, decisions, and the reasoning behind them foster a culture of trust and understanding. When leaders communicate openly, sharing successes and failures, they create an environment where team members feel valued and informed. This transparency encourages open dialogue and collaboration, as team members feel comfortable expressing their ideas and concerns without fear of judgment or reprisal. This open communication also extends to sharing organizational goals and challenges, allowing employees to align their efforts with the company's objectives.

Leaders who practice transparency are more likely to receive honest feedback from their team, which can lead to improved decision-making and problem-solving. Moreover, transparency in leadership helps to build credibility and accountability. When forthcoming about mistakes or setbacks, leaders demonstrate integrity and a willingness to learn. This approach can inspire team members to take ownership of their work and be more accountable for their actions. In today's digital age, transparency has become even more crucial. With information readily available, employees and stakeholders expect a higher level of openness from their leaders. Organizations that embrace transparency are often better equipped to navigate crises and maintain stakeholder trust during challenging times.

Jesus taught the importance of straightforward communication and avoiding deceitful speech. He speaks of the importance of maintaining integrity and transparency in our actions and the simplicity and honesty of communication. Matthew 5:37 says, *"All you need to say is simply 'Yes' or 'No'; anything beyond this comes from the evil one."* I have often seen a leader wanting to hide something from their team from the organization's confidentiality and start a stream of lies to cover up the truth. Sometimes, it is just best to tell them you are not at liberty to discuss the topic but assure them you will share what you know at the appropriate time, and everything will be alright.

Earlier in my career, I was running a group of cafeterias, and we were closing one down. We were operating the employee cafeteria for a company that was going bankrupt, and they could no longer provide this benefit to their employees. I knew we were about to sign a contract with another company, and I could utilize the manager and some of the staff in the new location. Due to not wanting to jeopardize the pending agreement, I had not told my staff what the plans were. One evening, while I was bowling with my sons in a youth and adult league, I received a call from my manager of this cafeteria. She was stressed over the looming closure. I distinctly remember her asking me, "How can you bowl at a time like this?" I told her not to worry. I had a position lined up for her, but I could not discuss it now due to confidentiality. I could continue to be honest in my communication without jeopardizing the project.

Ethical behavior is also essential in setting a positive example. Leaders who prioritize doing what is right demonstrate a commitment to fairness and justice, even when challenging or unpopular. By adhering to ethical standards and holding themselves accountable for their actions, leaders establish a culture of integrity and responsibility within their team.

I learned a valuable lesson about integrity early in life from my mom. I was around the age of 8-10 years old when my mom gave me a quarter to go to the corner store to buy some penny candy. This was back in the sixties when you could buy pieces of candy for a penny each. As I got to the store, I passed a vending machine selling drinks. As most kids did back then, I checked the change shute for any loose change someone may have accidentally left behind, as well as hitting the buttons to see if a drink would fall out. Lo and behold, that day, a drink came tumbling out of the machine. I enjoyed this special treat as I went home with my bag of candy.

My mom asked where I got the drink, knowing I had insufficient money. I told her what I had done, not knowing anything was wrong with it. She told me that I had not purchased it and needed to go back and pay the store for it. I insisted that "someone had paid for it.". But, she said, I had not. She gave me the money to go pay the clerk for the drink. When I got to the store and went to pay for it, the clerk refused my money, saying that the drink had already been paid for. I would not take no for an answer and insisted she take the money. I could not go back home without paying for the drink. That lesson has stuck with me for close to 60 years.

Proverbs 12:22 (NIV): *"The Lord detests lying lips, but he delights in people who are trustworthy."* This verse underscores the importance of honesty and integrity in ethical behavior.

Ultimately, leading by example is more than words; it's about embodying the values and behaviors you want to see in others. When leaders consistently demonstrate integrity, transparency, and ethical behavior, they inspire their team members to do the same, creating a culture of trust, accountability, and excellence.

Are you faithful to your word? I used to joke with some people I have worked with about telling the client or potential client everything they wanted to hear. There would be all sorts of promises made that the person knew could not be fulfilled. They figured that they would figure out a solution or not fulfill the promises and hope the client would not return and ask about it.

Solomon wrote the Book of Proverbs in the Bible. He was teaching the young people of his day the essential things in life, how to obtain wisdom, and how to lead a proper life. He was teaching them how to apply God's wisdom to their lives. Part of what he taught them was about personal relationships. That may be in the form of friends, coworkers, and family. This includes being trustworthy.

> *The LORD hates those who don't keep their word, but he delights and those who do.* Proverbs 12:22 (NLT)

Does this describe you? Are you one who makes all sorts of promises to make someone happy and does not worry about living up to your commitments? I have always believed in underpromising and overdelivering. There may be a request that I think I may be able to do, but I have a certain level of doubt about whether I can do it. I try to let the person know that my goal is to satisfy their request, but I need to do more research or brainstorm ideas on how to make it happen. I did not ignore their request but was honest in my approach.

Trust is the foundation of all successful relationships, whether personal or professional. Building trust within your team is crucial as a leader, creating an environment where individuals can thrive, take risks, and work together effectively. Consistently displaying honesty and trustworthiness is essential in establishing this foundation of trust. When your team sees you act with integrity, be transparent in your communication, and honor your commitments, they feel secure relying on you and confident in your leadership.

This consistency builds credibility and reliability and reinforces the trust your team has in you. In a trusting environment, team members feel safe taking risks and sharing their ideas without fear of judgment or reprisal. They know their contributions will be valued and respected and are more likely to engage actively in problem-solving and innovation. Trust encourages openness and collaboration, as individuals feel comfortable sharing their thoughts and perspectives, leading to richer discussions and more creative solutions.

Furthermore, trust enables effective teamwork by fostering a sense of cohesion and mutual support among team members. When individuals trust one another, they are more willing to collaborate, share responsibilities, and work towards common goals. This collaborative spirit strengthens the bonds within the team and enhances its overall performance.

Accountability is a crucial component of effective leadership, closely intertwined with trust. When leaders prioritize accountability, they demonstrate their commitment to the organization's goals and inspire confidence and respect from their team members. By holding themselves accountable for their actions and decisions, leaders set a powerful example for their team. Think back to when one of your managers/leaders of your organization acknowledged their errors or shortcomings. How did it make you feel? When leaders take ownership of their mistakes, admit when they've made errors, and actively work to rectify them, they show humility and integrity. This transparency builds trust within the team, as members see their leader as someone reliable and honest, even in the face of adversity. Does it make you more willing to proactively ask for help in your weaker areas? If you are willing to make mistakes, you will strive to accomplish greater things. In the end, your team will grow. If you try to hide your mistakes, your team will tend to do the same thing, thus bringing down the team.

Notice that I did not say to lower the standards. On the contrary, keep your standards high, reaching for the stars with unwavering determination. Embrace the journey of growth, allowing mistakes to become stepping stones on your path to greatness. These missteps are not failures but valuable lessons, shaping you into a stronger, more resilient individual. As you navigate the challenges of personal and professional development, remember that true growth often lies just beyond your comfort zone. If you find yourself effortlessly achieving your goals 100% of the time, take a moment to reflect. This ease might indicate you're not stretching yourself to your full potential. Dare to dream bigger, to push harder, and to inspire those around you to reach for seemingly impossible heights. You possess untapped reserves of strength and creativity waiting to be unleashed. By setting ambitious, even audacious goals, you ignite a fire within yourself and your team, spurring innovation and breakthrough performances. Remember, the greatest leaders and achievers in history didn't settle for mediocrity. They constantly challenged themselves and those around them to surpass expectations. You have that same power within you. Embrace the challenge, relish the journey, and let your unwavering commitment to excellence propel you towards extraordinary achievements.

When I speak of accountability, I do not discuss blame or punishment. Getting angry with people when they fall short is not a productive process for holding people accountable. It almost always reduces motivation and performance. Accountability is about delivering on a commitment. It's the responsibility to an outcome, not just a set of tasks. It's taking the initiative with thoughtful, strategic follow-through. Make sure you put everything into perspective. We will all make mistakes and will fall short of expectations at times. Developing your team means you lift someone when they are struggling. We help them overcome the shortfalls so the ultimate goals can be reached.

Part of holding someone accountable is knowing you have given them all the tools to be successful. The first step is to be crystal clear about what you expect. This means being transparent about the outcome you're looking for. It doesn't all have to come from you. The more skilled your people are, the more ideas and strategies should come from them. Have you given them the resources they need? It could be training, supplies, or as simple as having the task be attainable.

Many companies give their employees annual reviews. It is an assessment of their performance over the past twelve months and a chance to coach them on areas of weakness and set goals for the coming year. There should never be anything in the review you have not already discussed at some point with them. Do not wait until the review process to evaluate and coach your team. They deserve honest feedback throughout the year and can potentially improve in the weaker areas before the annual review time comes around.

Give them honest feedback on their performance. They should never be surprised if you end up at a point where you must let them go due to performance reasons. It would be best if you had been communicating with them all along the way. It may not be them who is the problem in the situation. By providing regular feedback, coaching, and support, leaders help individuals understand where they stand and how they can improve. This constructive approach to accountability fosters a continuous learning and development culture, where team members are encouraged to strive for excellence and take ownership of their professional growth.

Being a good leader isn't just about sticking to a plan. It's more like a journey where you're always learning and evolving. You start by knowing yourself inside and out, flaws and all. That self-awareness helps you see what you're great at and where you could use some work. And once you're tuned in like that, you can focus on growing and getting better every step of the way.

When leaders know what they're good at, they can use those strengths to motivate and uplift their team. By putting their strengths into action, whether making decisions or taking charge, they show they know their stuff and can be relied on, earning the respect of their crew. And when they're upfront about where they might need a hand, it's like they're saying, "Hey, I'm human too." That openness builds trust and lets others feel comfortable being honest, too.

Keeping on the path of self-improvement is critical to leading by example. It's all about staying curious, reflecting on what's what, and pushing yourself to improve. Leaders who are all about growth don't shy away from learning opportunities, whether it's a training course, a mentor's advice, or feedback from the team. They see setbacks as chances to learn and grow, not as roadblocks. By actively pursuing personal growth and development, leaders set a powerful example for their team members. They show that growth is a lifelong journey and that there is always room for improvement, regardless of experience level or expertise. This continuous improvement mindset inspires those around them to adopt a similar approach, creating a culture of learning and innovation within the team. Leading by example requires adapting and evolving in response to changing circumstances. Leaders who demonstrate flexibility and resilience in the face of challenges inspire confidence and motivate others to do the same. By modeling adaptability and perseverance, they show their team members that obstacles can be overcome and that success is attainable through persistence and determination.

Being a role model isn't just about one thing; it's a mix of being in tune with yourself, always looking to get better, and committing to growing personally. When leaders focus on improving themselves, it rubs off on everyone else, spurring them to step up their game, too. That vibe creates a culture where everyone aims for the stars and hits their targets.

Leadership influence plays a significant role in shaping team dynamics, extending far beyond mere directive authority. A leader's actions, decisions, and behaviors establish the overall tone and cultural framework for the entire team, creating a pervasive atmosphere that affects every aspect of team functioning. By leveraging this influence positively and consistently, leaders can effectively demonstrate and reinforce the crucial principles of trust and responsibility, setting a standard for all team members to aspire to. This approach tends to have a powerful ripple effect throughout the team, creating a cascading impact on team culture and performance. When team members observe their leader consistently embodying these values, they internalize and emulate them in their interactions and work processes. This process of social learning and modeling often leads to widespread adoption of similar attitudes and behaviors across the entire team, fostering a shared sense of purpose and ethical conduct.

A team operating with high levels of trust and responsibility will likely be more cohesive, resilient, and effective in its operations. This unified approach can significantly drive organizational success, as the team works collaboratively and synergistically towards common goals. The increased levels of trust enable more open communication, creative problem-solving, and mutual support among team members. At the same time, a strong sense of responsibility ensures that everyone takes ownership of their tasks and contributes meaningfully to the team's objectives. Ultimately, a leader's conscious and deliberate decision to model positive behaviors can transform team performance on multiple levels. It can enhance individual productivity, improve interpersonal relationships, and create a more positive and engaging work environment. This transformation can contribute substantially to achieving organizational objectives as the team becomes more aligned, motivated, and capable of tackling complex challenges. Effective leadership influence catalyzes organizational excellence, driving team and company success in an increasingly competitive business landscape.

Chapter 4

Nurturing Growth and Development

Supporting your team's success

Being a supportive leader is more than just overseeing projects and ensuring deadlines are met; it's about fostering an environment where each team member feels valued, supported, and empowered to grow personally and professionally. This involves taking on the role of a mentor and guide, actively investing in the growth and development of your team members to help them reach their fullest potential. Understand that each team member brings unique talents, skills, and aspirations. You must nurture these strengths while providing opportunities for growth and learning. This may involve offering constructive feedback, identifying areas for improvement, and providing resources or training to help team members develop new skills. I have heard people say that you should treat everyone the same. That is not true. Everyone is different, so you need to interact with them differently. What motivates one person will not necessarily motivate another. Focus on bringing each person up to their potential.

Look at how Jesus developed His team of disciples. What a diverse group of people they were. Each of them brought with them unique experiences, perspectives, and skills. Jesus did not try to do it alone. He built a diverse team and invested in their growth and development. He did not keep all the power to Himself but shared it with His disciples, giving them the authority to preach, heal, and cast out demons (Mark 3:14-15). Jesus always believed in empowering and delegating, which multiplied His leadership through His disciples.

The establishment of a trust-based culture with open communication channels characterizes supportive leadership. This environment encourages team members to seek guidance and freely express their ideas and concerns without fear of judgment or reprisal. As discussed in the previous chapter, the trust factor is crucial in fostering a supportive and collaborative atmosphere where individuals feel valued and respected. This leadership style promotes innovation, creativity, and practical problem-solving by creating a safe space for experimentation and risk-taking, ultimately contributing to the team's success and overall productivity.

A key aspect of supportive leadership is the provision of mentorship and guidance to team members. This involves several components that are essential for nurturing talent and fostering professional growth:

1. Sharing knowledge and expertise: Leaders actively impart their wisdom and experience, helping team members develop new skills and broaden their understanding of the industry or field.

2. Active listening to understand individual needs and aspirations: Supportive leaders pay close attention to their team members' concerns, goals, and ambitions, allowing for tailored support and development opportunities.
3. Offering personalized support and encouragement:

By recognizing each team member's unique strengths and challenges, leaders can provide targeted assistance and motivation to help individuals reach their full potential. By acting as a mentor, a supportive leader helps team members in various ways:

1. Navigate challenges: Providing guidance and perspective when faced with difficult situations or complex problems.
2. Overcome obstacles: Offering strategies and resources to help team members overcome barriers and setbacks.
3. Achieve their goals: Assisting in setting realistic objectives and creating actionable plans to reach personal and professional milestones.

This leadership approach ultimately facilitates team members' growth and development, fostering a sense of loyalty and commitment to the organization. Supportive leaders create an environment where individuals feel empowered to take on new responsibilities and stretch their capabilities, increasing job satisfaction and retention rates. Supportive leadership, therefore, not only benefits the immediate team dynamics but also contributes to the organization's long-term success and sustainability by cultivating skilled and confident team members. By investing in the development of their workforce, supportive leaders build a strong foundation for future growth and innovation, ensuring that the organization remains competitive and adaptable in an ever-changing business landscape. Too often, when we think of mentorship, we think of an experienced person teaching a newcomer in a field. We need to be open to the reverse as well. Your team may have some great ideas and expertise you are unaware of and can learn from. Keep an open mind.

In addition to mentorship, you should prioritize recognizing and celebrating your team members' achievements and contributions. Acknowledging their successes and showing appreciation for their efforts reinforces a sense of value and belonging within the team, motivating individuals to strive for excellence. Too often, we point out the negatives and shortfalls and do not give enough recognition for what they are doing right.

According to a CNBC survey on workplace happiness, more than 9 in 10 workers (91%) who have a mentor at work report feeling satisfied with their jobs, including a majority (57%) who feel "very satisfied." This same group is also more likely to feel happy with their compensation and appreciated by colleagues than those without a workplace coach. Sometimes unhappy workers need more guidance than their boss can provide. Having a mentor to provide feedback, advice, and prospective opportunities is a massive advantage for any employee. Companies benefit from mentorship, too, as workers are less likely to quit when they say they have someone at work who they consider to be a mentor.[iv]

It's important to note that workplace mentors can come from any level and branch of the organizational chart. Some mentors are senior leaders shepherding more junior leaders or managers in an executive mentoring program. Some mentors are new hires or younger associates who practice reverse or reciprocal mentoring to educate more tenured employees on contemporary tools like social media or AI. Reverse and reciprocal mentoring can also go beyond workplace tools and skills to address broader gaps between employees of different generations or backgrounds in communication and culture. Some companies may use employees to mentor local students, connect employees as part of diversity networks, or even help their diverse suppliers improve and grow as small businesses.[v]

One effective way to promote a learning culture is by providing access to resources and training opportunities. This may include offering access to online courses, workshops, seminars, or industry conferences relevant to the team's goals and objectives. By investing in these resources, you demonstrate your commitment to supporting the growth and development of your team members and provide them with the tools they need to expand their skills and knowledge base.

Encourage team members to share their expertise, experiences, and best practices with one another through regular meetings, brainstorming sessions, or collaborative projects. This allows individuals to learn from each other's successes and challenges and fosters a sense of camaraderie and teamwork within the team.

As a leader, it's essential to lead by example by actively participating in and promoting learning and development initiatives. This may involve setting aside time for your professional growth, sharing insights and lessons learned with your team, and demonstrating a willingness to learn from others. By modeling a commitment to continuous learning, you inspire your team members to follow suit and create a culture where growth and development are valued and prioritized. Remember that supporting your team's success is not just about achieving short-term goals. It's about investing in their long-term growth and well-being. A supportive leadership style inspires team members to push their boundaries, take risks, and embrace new challenges.

Have you heard anyone say, "If I want it done right, I must do it myself?" What does that say about them? Are they unwilling to trust a teammate with a task? Are they perfectionists? You must be willing to delegate duties for the team to grow. Sure, they may make mistakes, but that is fine. You were not perfect at it when you did it the first time. They may have more talent in that area than you do and may improve on it more than you could imagine.

I am far from the best at most things my team is tasked to accomplish, and I am no less of a leader because of it. Too often, we feel the leader must be the team's most talented person. The leader needs to bring out the best in their team. Utilize all the team members' strengths. As a catering manager, I could create a theme for a party and create the menu around the theme, but decorating for it was not in my wheelhouse of talents. I would paint my vision and let the team run with it.

I played trumpet in the band in school. Many instruments make various sounds and melodies, working together to perform a piece of music. All instruments have their role in the overall music. Some stand out, and some are in the background complimenting the others, but they all have an

LEADING BY SERVING ~ 35

essential role. The same happens within your team. Bring out all the individual talents to take the team's performance to higher levels.

We can learn this lesson from 1 Corinthians 12:14-27 (NLT)

Yes, the body has many different parts, not just one part. If the foot says, "I am not a part of the body because I am not a hand," that does not make it any less a part of the body. And if the ear says, "I am not part of the body because I am not an eye," would that make it any less a part of the body? If the whole body were an eye, how would you hear? Or if your whole body were an ear, how would you smell anything?

But our bodies have many parts, and God has put each part just where he wants it. How strange a body would be if it had only one part! Yes, there are many parts, but only one body. The eye can never say to the hand, "I don't need you." The head can't say to the feet, "I don't need you."

In fact, some parts of the body that seem weakest and least important are actually the most necessary. And the parts we regard as less honorable are those we clothe with the greatest care. So we carefully protect those parts that should not be seen, while the more honorable parts do not require this special care. So God has put the body together such that extra honor and care are given to those parts that have less dignity. This makes for harmony among the members, so that all the members care for each other. If one part suffers, all the parts suffer with it, and if one part is honored, all the parts are glad.

All of you together are Christ's body, and each of you is a part of it.

As you let each of them shine through their talents, learn from them. In the early 1980s, I worked for Domino's Pizza. At the time, their main promotional approach was 30 minutes of free delivery. If they did not deliver your pizza to your door in less than 30 minutes, you got it for free. As a college student, I hoped they would take just a bit too long so I could save some money, but now I was on the other end of the transaction. I was managing a store, and we needed to make a profit.

One hectic Friday night, I remember hearing the order taker tell the customer about the delay and that it would be free. She did not stop there. She proceeded to "up-sell" drinks to go with the order. She asked them if they would like to add any sodas to the order and let them know they would also be free. What a concept! Now you think that this is the craziest thing in the world, but I think that it is brilliant. Look at it from the eyes of the customer. What were their thoughts when they were honestly told about the delay, promised that there would be no charge as our apology, and then offered something extra for no apparent reason and no cost as well? Would you be a repeat restaurant customer if treated that way?

After about a month, we no longer gave away pizzas because we were fully staffed with strong employees who bonded as a team toward the shared vision. We doubled the sales within three months and never looked back. I ended up training two assistant managers to the point that they were promoted to their own stores from this location. We then operated in a stress-free work environment. I did not put pressure on them to not deliver pizzas late. That was not part of the vision. The vision was to give excellent customer service (even if there was a cost) so that the customers would become loyal to us.

This empowerment of the employees to do what it takes to reach that goal inspired my order taker to do what she did that busy Friday night. Picture a service staff member asked by a customer if they can get a variation of their meal that was not listed on the menu. If you had not empowered them to take care of the customer, their answer might have been, "I am sorry, but that option is not available." The customer would have ordered something else or settled for what was available. Now, let's look at the empowered server. They would have taken it upon themselves to work with the cook to satisfy the customer's request. Ultimately, the client walks away with an exceptional experience, becomes a regular customer, and promotes your business in conversations with friends. The unsatisfied customer will also talk about your business to their friends, but not in the same light. Give them a mission to accomplish. In this case, an exceptional dining experience empowered them to make it happen.

When individuals clearly understand their contributions' impact on the organization, they are more likely to feel invested in their work and motivated to perform at their best. It is essential to actively engage with team members to help them connect the dots between their daily tasks and the company's overarching objectives. Think of your team as a sports team. Everyone has their position to play. In baseball, it may be the pitcher, catcher, shortstop, or outfielder. They may not be involved in every play, but they are all needed to be successful. They may not be front and center and get all the attention, but they are equally important. We need all their talents and performance to bring the team together for the final product. This can be achieved through regular communication and recognition of both small milestones and the broader context in which they occur.

Acknowledging and celebrating minor victories along the journey is a practical approach to fostering team success. By recognizing the incremental progress made by team members, leaders reinforce the value of individual contributions and maintain high morale within the group. This strategy goes beyond simply boosting motivation; it enhances the team's collective sense of accomplishment and purpose, creating a positive feedback loop that drives further success.

Effective leaders understand the power of frequent, small-scale recognition. Instead of waiting solely for significant milestones or major accomplishments to praise team members, they actively seek out and highlight the small wins that occur daily or weekly. These seemingly minor achievements, when acknowledged, create a cumulative effect that builds momentum and drives the team towards larger goals. Recognizing small victories can take various forms, such as verbal praise during team meetings, written commendations in company newsletters, or even small rewards or incentives.

This approach keeps team members engaged and motivated and helps maintain focus on the overarching objectives. Remember, it's the accumulation of these small wins that ultimately leads to major accomplishments. Leaders can create a more resilient, motivated, and high-performing team capable of achieving remarkable results by cultivating an environment that recognizes and values progress at all levels.

Chapter 5

The Upside Down Organizational Chart

Changing your perspective

Imagine a world where leadership isn't about power but about empowerment. This is the transformative vision of servant leadership, a revolutionary approach that turns the traditional hierarchy on its head and unlocks the true potential of every individual within an organization.

Picture a workplace where your voice matters, your contributions are celebrated, and you're not just an employee but a valued member of a thriving community. This isn't just a dream – it's the reality that servant leadership can create!

By placing front-line workers at the pinnacle of the organizational structure, we're not just challenging convention; we're igniting a spark of innovation that can set the entire company ablaze with creativity and passion. When leaders serve their teams, they're not diminishing their own importance – they're multiplying the strength and capabilities of the entire organization.

Think of the possibilities when every team member feels empowered to share their ideas, collaboration flows freely, and the collective wisdom of the entire workforce is harnessed. This is the power of servant leadership—a catalyst for unprecedented engagement, satisfaction, and innovation.

As we embrace this revolutionary approach, we're not just changing our organizational charts – we're reshaping the very fabric of our work culture. We're creating an environment where every individual can thrive, where potential is unleashed, and where the boundaries of what's possible are constantly expanded.

This shift in perspective creates a ripple effect of positivity, innovation, and dedication throughout the entire organization. Like a pebble thrown into a still pond, the impact of servant leadership spreads far and wide, touching every corner of the company culture. By inverting the traditional hierarchy, we unlock the true potential of our workforce. Front-line employees, who are closest to customers and daily operations, gain the platform to share their insights and ideas. Their voices become catalysts for positive change, driving the company forward with fresh perspectives and ground-level expertise. It's as if we're tapping into a wellspring of creativity and knowledge that has always been there, just waiting to be unleashed. Embracing this upside-down approach isn't just about reshuffling titles; it's about reimagining the very essence of leadership.

When leaders focus on removing obstacles, nurturing growth, and championing their team's success, they create an environment where everyone can thrive. This servant leadership mindset fosters loyalty, boosts morale, and ignites a shared passion for excellence. It's like planting a seed of empowerment that grows into a mighty oak of collective achievement. Let's dare to turn our organizations upside down and witness the transformative power of putting our teams first.

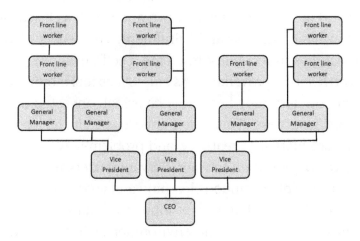

By serving those who serve our customers, we can build stronger, more resilient, and ultimately more successful businesses. The future belongs to those who recognize true leadership means lifting others up and paving the way for collective triumph. It's time to embrace this paradigm shift and embark on a journey of organizational transformation that will inspire future generations. Imagine the possibilities when every team member feels valued, supported, and empowered. Picture a workplace where ideas flow freely, innovation thrives, and collaboration knows no bounds. This is the promise of servant leadership – a beacon of hope in a world hungry for meaningful change.

Together, we can rewrite the rules of organizational success and create a legacy of empowerment that will resonate for years to come. The time for change is now, and the power to make it happen lies within each of us. Let's turn the world of business upside down and watch as it reaches new heights of success and fulfillment. The beauty of this approach lies in its ability to create a self-sustaining cycle of growth and improvement. As employees feel more valued and empowered, they become increasingly invested in the company's success. This heightened engagement leads to greater productivity, creativity, and problem-solving, which drives the organization forward. Servant leadership also fosters a culture of continuous learning and adaptability.

When leaders actively seek input from all levels of the organization, they create an environment where new ideas are welcomed and innovation flourishes. This agility becomes a powerful competitive advantage in today's rapidly changing business landscape. This inverted model of leadership has the potential to transform not just individual companies but entire industries. As organizations embracing servant leadership outperform their competitors, others will notice and follow suit. This ripple effect could lead to a widespread shift in corporate culture, creating a more humane and fulfilling work environment for millions worldwide. The impact of servant leadership extends beyond the workplace, touching the lives of employees' families and communities.

When individuals feel fulfilled and valued at work, they bring that positive energy home, creating a virtuous cycle of well-being that radiates outward. As we stand on the brink of this leadership revolution, we must remember that change begins with each of us. Every interaction, every decision, and every gesture of support contributes to this new paradigm. We build a brighter, more collaborative future by committing to serve others and elevate those around us. Let us embrace this challenge with open hearts and minds, knowing that the journey may be challenging, but the rewards are immeasurable. Together, we can transform workplaces into vibrant communities where creativity flourishes, innovation thrives, and human potential is unleashed.

This shift requires courage, empathy, and a willingness to challenge the status quo. As leaders, we must cultivate an environment of trust, where vulnerability is seen as strength and diverse perspectives are celebrated. By fostering genuine connections and nurturing the growth of our teams, we create a ripple effect that extends far beyond office walls. Imagine a world where everyone feels empowered to bring their authentic self to work, collaboration replaces competition, and success is measured in profits and our positive impact on people's lives.

This transformative vision is not just a distant dream but a tangible reality within our grasp. However, it demands our unwavering commitment, steadfast dedication, and consistent daily practice to bring it to fruition. Through our actions and decisions, we can vividly demonstrate the profound power and impact of servant leadership, inspiring those around us to embrace this noble philosophy. As we wholeheartedly embrace this new paradigm, we are not merely changing our own lives but are actively shaping the future. With every compassionate act, every innovative idea, and every selfless decision, we lay the foundation for a more empathetic, dynamic, and fulfilling professional landscape. This ripple effect extends far beyond the confines of our organizations, touching lives and transforming communities. Together, we have the extraordinary opportunity to create a world where leadership is synonymous with service, where innovation is driven by empathy, and where success is measured not just in profits but in the positive impact we make on others.

Chapter 6

Cultivating Collaboration

Harnessing the Power of Teamwork

The adage "teamwork makes the dream work" holds true in the dynamic business landscape. Rarely does success manifest solely from the efforts of a single individual; instead, it emerges from the collective synergy and collaboration of a cohesive team. Embracing a collaborative leadership approach unlocks the vast potential of team members, harnessing their diverse skills, perspectives, and creativity to drive innovation and elevate productivity to new heights.

> Two are better than one, because they have a good return for their labor: If either of them falls down, one can help the other up. But pity anyone who falls and has no one to help them up. Ecclesiastes 4:9-10 (NIV)

Encouraging team collaboration transcends mere task delegation; it necessitates cultivating an environment conducive to open communication, mutual respect, and unwavering trust. The fertile soil for genuine collaboration is nurtured when team members feel empowered to freely express their ideas and opinions without the looming specter of judgment. Servant leaders understand the inherent strength of collaborative efforts within a team. They recognize that by fostering an environment of collaboration, individuals can thrive collectively, achieving tremendous success and fulfillment personally and organizationally.

Servant leaders promote collaboration by providing each team member with the space to grow and develop professionally. This may involve offering opportunities for skill-building, training, and mentorship, allowing individuals to expand their capabilities and contribute more effectively to the team's goals. By investing in the growth and development of each team member, servant leaders empower individuals to bring their best selves to the table, enriching the collective experience and enhancing overall team performance.

Team leadership strategies significantly impact workplace dynamics and productivity, shaping an organization's performance and culture. Effective leaders create platforms for team members to showcase their strengths and talents, recognizing that everyone brings unique skills and perspectives. This approach maximizes the team's potential and fosters a sense of empowerment and engagement among employees. Regular recognition and celebration of individual achievements are crucial in fostering a culture of appreciation.

Acknowledging small wins and major accomplishments, leaders boost morale and motivation while promoting camaraderie and mutual respect. This practice encourages team members to support one another's successes, creating a positive feedback loop that enhances overall team performance. Encouraging a supportive group dynamic is crucial for long-term success. This involves promoting open communication, trust, and transparency within the team. Leaders who prioritize these elements create an environment where team members feel comfortable expressing their thoughts, concerns, and ideas without fear of judgment or reprisal. Such an atmosphere of psychological safety allows members to freely share ideas, seek assistance, and collaborate on projects, leading to increased innovation and problem-solving capabilities.

This unity enhances team cohesion and resilience, enabling the group to effectively overcome challenges and achieve collective goals. When team members feel supported and valued, they are more likely to go above and beyond in their roles, contributing to their overall success. One practical method to promote teamwork is through team-building activities conducted virtually or in person. These activities allow team members to bond outside the traditional work environment, enhancing morale, improving collaboration, and strengthening communication. Team-building exercises can range from simple icebreakers to more complex problem-solving challenges to foster connections and mutual understanding among team members.

By implementing these strategies, leaders can create a more cohesive, motivated, and productive team environment. This approach benefits individual team members by enhancing job satisfaction and personal growth, contributing to the organization's overall success. A well-led team is more adaptable, innovative, and capable of meeting the ever-changing demands of today's business landscape. Moreover, effective team leadership strategies can improve employee retention rates, as team members are more likely to remain committed to an organization where they feel valued and supported.

Creating an open vibe where everyone chats freely is key to teaming up well. Leaders play a big role by setting up ways for their teams to talk openly and really listen to each other. These back-and-forth conversations spark fresh ideas and ensure everyone feels included and heard. Plus, respecting each other is super essential for good teamwork. When team members admire and appreciate what everyone brings, collaboration rocks. It's all about celebrating differences and making everyone feel valued, which makes our teamwork richer and more fun!

Trust is like the solid ground that holds up successful collaboration. When team members trust each other fully, they are more willing to take risks, share tasks, and rely on each other. If you are a trusted leader, your employees will feel empowered to share their ideas and opinions even when they differ from yours. Because employees aren't afraid to speak up, you'll become privy to different perspectives, perhaps discovering new ideas or solutions. Individuals are likelier to change their behaviors when their manager has built trust. Mistrust breeds fear, disengagement, lack of loyalty, diminished returns on investment, and reduced productivity. Team performance will suffer without trust because you can't operate efficiently. Employees will have trouble making decisions or admitting mistakes, fearing negative repercussions if they do. On the other hand, when you've

LEADING BY SERVING ~ 49

developed trust, staff can seek guidance and support without fear. In a fearful environment, employees will wait to admit mistakes, often causing more problems than if they'd spoken up sooner. In a trusting environment, employees aren't afraid to own up to mistakes and bring solutions. This limits the fallout of an error and allows the employee to view the error as a learning opportunity.[vi]

Promoting team collaboration and synergy requires more than assigning tasks; cultivating an environment characterized by open communication, mutual respect, and unwavering trust. By embracing these principles, leaders unlock their teams' full potential, propelling them toward shared goals and realizing unparalleled success through collective effort.

Inclusivity is a cornerstone of effective teamwork. It catalyzes a collaborative environment where everyone feels welcomed and valued for their distinctive contributions. When each team member experiences a genuine sense of belonging, they are naturally inclined to engage more actively in collaborative endeavors, fueling the team's collective synergy.

Embracing diversity in backgrounds, perspectives, and skills within our teams is paramount to unlocking the full potential of collaborative efforts. Each team member brings unique experiences, knowledge, and viewpoints, enriching the collective pool of ideas and possibilities. By embracing this diversity, we open the door to a wealth of fresh insights and innovative approaches to problem-solving. Too often, we think of diversity in the workplace regarding a person's race. We are diverse in so many ways. Someone in their twenties brings different perspectives and ideas than those in their fifties and sixties. A college graduate brings different skills than someone who has been in the industry for many years without a degree. No one is more valuable to the team than each other. It is the combining of all these skills and perspectives that allow us to grow even stronger as a team.

Inclusivity fosters a mutual respect and appreciation culture, where each team member is recognized for their unique strengths and contributions. When individuals feel valued and respected for their diverse skills and perspectives, they are empowered to engage in collaborative endeavors fully, leveraging their unique talents to propel the team toward success. Inclusive teamwork also promotes psychological safety, where team members feel comfortable expressing their ideas and opinions without fear of judgment or reprisal. This psychological safety creates a supportive environment conducive to open communication, constructive feedback, and productive collaboration.

Ultimately, inclusivity is not merely a buzzword but a fundamental principle underpinning effective teamwork. By embracing diversity and fostering an environment where everyone feels valued and respected, we unlock the potential for innovation, creativity, and collective achievement that propels our teams to unparalleled success. Remember that collaboration is not just about achieving goals; it's about building relationships based on trust and support. By harnessing the power of teamwork, we can create a harmonious work environment where each member feels empowered to contribute their best selves towards shared success. Together, we can achieve greatness beyond what any one person could accomplish alone.

Chapter 7

Developing your Team Members

Nurturing Growth

One of the hallmark traits of servant leadership is the unwavering commitment to fostering team members' professional and personal growth. This noble approach to leadership recognizes that investing in the development of individuals not only enhances their capabilities but also strengthens the collective capacity of the entire group. It's a powerful philosophy that can transform organizations and inspire greatness in others.

Servant leaders, like beacons of light guiding ships through stormy seas, understand the profound impact of nurturing their team's potential. They create an environment where growth is encouraged and celebrated, where each team member's journey of self-improvement becomes a shared triumph. This dedication to growth is akin to tending a garden - with careful nurturing and patience, even the smallest seedling can blossom into a magnificent tree.

These visionary leaders facilitate growth by providing ample opportunities for team members to spread their wings and soar. They open doors to leadership roles within group projects, trusting in their team's abilities and potential.

Servant leaders cultivate a rich soil of accountability, ownership, and skill development by delegating responsibilities and empowering individuals to lead initiatives. This hands-on experience is like a crucible, forging stronger, more confident leaders ready to face any challenge. Imagine a workplace where every day brings new opportunities to grow, where each challenge is seen as a stepping stone to greatness. This is the world that servant leaders create. They actively support their team members' ongoing education and development, encouraging them to drink deeply from the well of knowledge.

Whether attending conferences that spark innovation, enrolling in courses that expand horizons, or pursuing certifications that validate expertise, these leaders provide the needed resources and guidance. But the true magic of servant leadership lies in its personalized approach. These leaders are like skilled sculptors, carefully chiseling away at the marble to reveal the masterpiece within each team member. They seek to understand their team's unique goals and aspirations through regular communication and feedback. With this invaluable knowledge, servant leaders craft bespoke development plans that align with individual dreams and organizational needs. It's like composing a symphony where each instrument plays its unique part, contributing to a harmonious and inspiring whole.

This tailored approach optimizes individual growth and creates a workplace where personal fulfillment and professional success are intertwined. The impact of this leadership style ripples far beyond the individual. When team members feel their aspirations are acknowledged and supported, they become beacons of enthusiasm and dedication. Their engagement soars, and they strive for excellence for themselves and the entire team. It's like lighting a candle and watching its flame ignite countless others, creating a brilliant glow of collective achievement.

In essence, servant leadership is about believing in the potential of others and committing wholeheartedly to their growth. It's about creating a legacy of empowerment, where each person touched by this leadership style becomes a torchbearer, ready to light the way for others. As we embrace this inspiring approach, we build better teams and cultivate a brighter future, one empowered individual at a time. This transformative approach to leadership extends beyond the workplace, influencing the very fabric of society.

As servant leaders nurture growth within their teams, they inadvertently sow seeds of positive change in communities and families. The ripple effect of this leadership style creates waves of empowerment that wash over every aspect of life, fostering a culture of continuous improvement and mutual support. Servant leaders understand that true growth often requires stepping out of their comfort zones. They create safe spaces for experimentation and risk-taking, where failure is viewed not as a setback but as a valuable learning opportunity. This mindset shift transforms challenges into stepping stones, encouraging team members to embrace adversity with resilience and determination.

The impact of servant leadership on organizational culture is profound. It cultivates an atmosphere of trust, transparency, and mutual respect. Team members feel valued for their contributions and their inherent worth as individuals.

This sense of belonging and appreciation fuels a passion for excellence beyond mere job satisfaction, inspiring a deep-seated commitment to the organization's mission and values. The leaders recognize that growth is a holistic process, encompassing professional skills, emotional intelligence, interpersonal relationships, and overall well-being. They encourage work-life balance, promoting practices that nourish the mind, body, and spirit.

This comprehensive approach to development creates well-rounded individuals who are skilled professionals and compassionate, empathetic human beings. As organizations embrace servant leadership, they become incubators of innovation and creativity. The supportive environment allows ideas to flourish, encouraging team members to think outside the box and propose novel solutions. This culture of innovation becomes a competitive advantage, propelling the organization to new heights of success and influence. Ultimately, the commitment to growth inherent in servant leadership is an investment in the future that extends far beyond the tenure of any single leader.

As team members grow and evolve, they, too, become servant leaders, perpetuating a cycle of positive influence that can transform entire industries and societies. It reminds us of the incredible potential that lies within each individual and the transformative power of believing in others. As we continue to embrace and practice this inspiring leadership style, we pave the way for a brighter, more empowered future – one where everyone can grow, thrive, and make a meaningful difference in the world.

Chapter 8

The Ripple Effect of Servant Leadership

Making a Positive Impact Beyond the Workplace

Servant leadership is a transformative force that extends far beyond the confines of the workplace, creating a powerful ripple effect that resonates throughout society. When leaders wholeheartedly embrace the philosophy of serving others, they become catalysts for positive change, igniting a spark that illuminates not only their immediate environments but also the world at large. This selfless approach to leadership has the potential to inspire and uplift countless individuals, fostering a culture of compassion, empathy, and mutual support.

Our personal and professional lives are intricately woven together, forming a tapestry of experiences that shape our very essence. The rich tapestry of experiences we accumulate outside of work profoundly influences our leadership style, infusing it with depth, wisdom, and authenticity. Simultaneously, the leadership skills we cultivate in our professional roles seep into our personal lives, enhancing our relationships and interactions beyond the office walls. The challenges we face in our personal lives are not isolated; they ripple outward, directly impacting our work performance and behavior. When we navigate personal difficulties, it can affect our focus, energy, and decision-making abilities in the workplace.

However, these challenges also present opportunities for growth, resilience, and empathy, ultimately strengthening our leadership capabilities. Conversely, the sense of personal fulfillment and contentment we cultivate in our lives outside of work acts as a wellspring of positive energy, fueling our professional endeavors with passion and purpose. When we find joy, balance, and meaning in our personal lives, it radiates through our work, inspiring creativity, boosting productivity, and fostering a more positive work environment for those around us. This interconnectedness reminds us that true success and fulfillment come from nurturing both our personal and professional selves, creating a harmonious balance that allows us to thrive in all aspects of life.

To be effective leaders, we must prioritize self-care, both physically and mentally. Taking care of ourselves allows us to better care for those who depend on us. Moreover, when we set an example by prioritizing our own well-being, we send a powerful message to our team members that self-care is essential and should be valued. This is why mindset and learning how to manage your mind is not a nice to do today, it is a must.

Our personal lives also have a significant influence on our business relationships. Consider a scenario where one of your employees is going through a challenging situation outside of work. It's likely that this employee will be preoccupied with their personal matters, leading to a decline in their usual performance. As their leader, it is our responsibility to understand their circumstances and provide the necessary support to help them navigate through this difficult time. By doing so, we not only assist them as individuals, but we also enable them to contribute more effectively to the team.[vii]

By extending their servant leadership principles beyond the workplace and into the community, individuals become beacons of inspiration, lighting the path for others to follow suit and embrace the ethos of servant leadership themselves. This transformative effect creates a powerful chain reaction of compassion, empathy, and selflessness that has the potential to reshape entire communities from the ground up.

A servant leader embodies a unique and transformative approach to leadership, characterized by their commitment to sharing power and prioritizing the needs of their employees above their own. This leadership philosophy emphasizes the importance of nurturing and empowering team members, fostering an environment where individuals can flourish personally and professionally. By focusing on the growth and well-being of their staff, servant leaders cultivate a workforce that is motivated, engaged, and equipped to perform at their highest potential.

This leadership style is firmly rooted in ethical principles and demonstrates a deep sense of empathy towards others. Servant leaders actively listen to their team members, show genuine concern for their welfare, and strive to create a supportive atmosphere that encourages open communication and mutual trust. They recognize that by investing in their employee's development and success, they are ultimately contributing to the overall strength and resilience of the organization. Research and real-world examples have consistently shown that servant leadership is not just a noble ideal but a highly effective approach that yields tangible benefits in the workplace.

Organizations led by servant leaders often experience increased productivity, as employees feel valued and motivated to give their best effort. Furthermore, this leadership style fosters a collaborative culture where team members are more likely to support one another and work cohesively towards common goals. The result is a more harmonious, innovative, and successful work environment that can adapt to challenges and thrive in today's dynamic business landscape.

For example, take John Robert Lewis, who, in 1958, wrote a letter to Dr. Martin Luther King Jr. In response, he received a round-trip bus ticket to Montgomery, Alabama. Upon his arrival, the 18-year-old Lewis was taken to First Baptist Church and ushered into King's office. This meeting sparked a relationship that would see numerous arrests, jailings, and severe beatings in a joint effort to obtain equal rights. Lewis went on to achieve great things with the guidance of King, who was a servant leader. Due to King's influence, Lewis became a prominent figure in the American civil rights movement and served as a United States congressman, thus inspiring a new generation of servant leaders.[viii]

As the story above demonstrates, servant leadership is an infinite loop of positive influence that develops strong leaders by serving the needs of others first. The power of servant leadership lies in its ability to inspire and empower individuals to reach their full potential, fostering a culture of trust and sustainable growth.

Servant leaders who actively engage in community service and outreach initiatives serve as living embodiments of their values, demonstrating through their actions the profound impact that servant leadership can have on society. Whether through volunteering, philanthropy, or grassroots advocacy efforts, these leaders sow the seeds of positive change, fostering a culture of altruism and social responsibility that permeates every facet of community life.

The ripple effect of servant leadership extends beyond individual actions, inspiring collective movements and collaborative endeavors aimed at addressing systemic issues and effecting meaningful societal change. By uniting individuals and organizations under a shared commitment to serving others, servant leaders galvanize communities to work together toward common goals, leveraging their collective strengths to tackle pressing challenges and build a brighter, more equitable future for all.

Servant leadership catalyzes a virtuous cycle of empowerment and upliftment. Acts of service inspire others to pay it forward, creating a ripple effect of compassion and generosity that knows no bounds. By embracing the philosophy of serving others and leading by example, individuals can harness the transformative power of servant leadership to make a lasting and meaningful impact on the world around them.

Leading by example and prioritizing the needs of others ignites a transformative spark within those we influence. It transcends the conventional notions of leadership centered on power and authority, instead emphasizing the profound impact that genuine care and selflessness can have on the lives of others. By embodying the principles of servant leadership, we not only inspire but also empower those around us to recognize their capacity for leadership and positive change.

Servant leadership holds immense potential for catalyzing meaningful societal change. Emphasizing empathy, compassion, and service fosters a culture of collaboration, cooperation, and collective action. In such an environment, individuals are encouraged to work together toward shared goals, drawing upon their diverse talents and perspectives to address pressing social issues and effect positive transformation.

This leadership style cultivates trust, respect, and inclusivity, where every voice is heard, valued, and respected. By prioritizing the needs of others and demonstrating a genuine commitment to their well-being, leaders create a sense of belonging and community that transcends individual differences and fosters unity and cohesion.

This approach promotes social responsibility by instilling a sense of duty and accountability toward the broader community. Leaders who prioritize the needs of others inspire a spirit of generosity and altruism among their followers, encouraging them to actively engage in service-oriented activities and contribute to the betterment of society.

Servant leadership is a powerful catalyst for positive change, both on an individual and societal level. By exemplifying humility, empathy, and a steadfast commitment to serving others, leaders create an environment where everyone is empowered to thrive and contribute to the greater good. Through collaboration, trust, and a shared sense of responsibility, servant leaders pave the way for a more compassionate, inclusive, and equitable society.

Imagine a world where every leader wholeheartedly embraces the principles of servant leadership, unlocking the boundless potential for transformative change and collective upliftment across societies. In this visionary landscape, the traditional hierarchical power structures are replaced by a more egalitarian approach, fostering mutual growth and shared success.

Leaders, driven by an unwavering commitment to the well-being of others, become catalysts for positive change, inspiring those around them to reach new heights of achievement and personal fulfillment. Picture a global community where individuals are no longer primarily motivated by self-interest or the relentless pursuit of power and status. Instead, they are guided by a deep-seated commitment to serving others with genuine passion and unwavering dedication. This paradigm shift in leadership philosophy creates a ripple effect, permeating all levels of society and fundamentally altering the dynamics of human interaction. In this reimagined world, empathy, compassion, and altruism become the cornerstones of decision-making processes, leading to more equitable and sustainable outcomes for all.

In such a world, communities thrive as servant leaders cultivate environments of collaboration, compassion, and empowerment. These leaders inspire a shared sense of purpose, rallying individuals around common goals and fostering a spirit of unity and cooperation. Through their selfless actions and unwavering commitment to the well-being of others, they ignite a ripple effect of positive change that reverberates throughout society.

Stronger communities emerge as servant leaders nurture environments where every voice is heard, valued, and respected. By prioritizing the needs of others and fostering a culture of inclusivity and belonging, they create spaces where individuals feel empowered to contribute their unique talents and perspectives to the collective good. This sense of ownership and agency fosters a deep understanding of connection and belonging, strengthening the social fabric and fostering resilience in the face of challenges.

Empowered individuals emerge as servant leaders and inspire others to recognize their potential for leadership and positive impact. By leading by example and demonstrating the transformative power of servant leadership, they encourage others to step forward, take initiative, and become catalysts for change. This empowerment fuels individual growth and development and amplifies the collective capacity for innovation, creativity, and problem-solving.

Ultimately, the impact is immeasurable in a world where servant leadership reigns supreme. Communities flourish, individuals thrive, and a collective sense of purpose emerges, driving humanity toward a brighter, more compassionate future. By embracing the principles of servant leadership and committing to serving others with passion and dedication, leaders pave the way for a world where the potential for positive change knows no bounds.

Our community is so important in our lives. Helen Keller once said, "Alone, we can do so little; together, we can do so much."[ix]

We can apply all the traits of a servant leader to being a community leader. You need to understand your community. Although we commonly think of community in terms of geographic proximity, people don't need to live close to one another to come together as a cohesive group. Thanks to modern technology, communities can now form over tremendous physical distances. Through customs, backgrounds, interests, and skills, countless commonalities can establish strong ties that bind people into close-knit communities.

Your job as a community leader is to know what values lie at the heart of your community. To make informed decisions, you must also foster and maintain a clear understanding of the various environmental and sociopolitical forces and all sides of the major issues affecting that community.

Quality servant leadership is virtually impossible without integrity and accountability. Your capabilities as a community leader are only as powerful as your reputation. Thus, you must do all possible to foster and enhance trust among stakeholders and community members. Lead with an emphasis on personal credibility by remaining transparent in all your actions and taking responsibility for your mistakes.

Diversity demands inclusivity. This means encouraging participation and involvement with all community members and ensuring all key stakeholders are at the table, including underrepresented community members. If you can't foster inclusion and consensus, you will unlikely go far as a community leader. A great way to accomplish this is to embrace hands-on leadership: try to guide groups rather than push them. "Aim to work side by side with them," recommends the Indeed Career Guide.[x] "If this means long hours or learning new skills, as the leader, you can set the example by doing these things alongside your team."

A one-size-fits-all approach to leading and interacting with diverse community members and stakeholders won't work. To better meet community needs and evolve with the times, you must remain open-minded and adaptable in your project management and decision-making. Of course, effective communication and collaboration with community members and other stakeholders are crucial to this endeavor.

Another powerful driver of confidence and self-assurance is self-reflection. Without substantial self-reflection, you cannot gain a true understanding of yourself, your leadership characteristics, or your ability to affect others. To put it a different way, you can't influence others if you don't understand them, and you cannot understand others if you don't understand yourself. Leaders with greater levels of self-awareness tend to foster healthier work environments, work more efficiently with team members, and make better decisions.[xi]

Chapter 9

Self-evaluation

Am I true to my beliefs?

Servant leadership thrives on a foundation of openness and receptivity to feedback. It recognizes that continuous self-awareness and growth are essential for effective leadership. Servant leaders understand that positive or constructive feedback is a valuable tool for personal and professional development, enabling them to refine their leadership skills and enhance their ability to serve their team effectively.

By actively seeking and encouraging feedback from their team and others within the organization, servant leaders demonstrate humility and a willingness to learn from others. They understand that every interaction provides an opportunity for growth and improvement, and they embrace feedback to deepen their understanding of themselves and their impact on others. This open and receptive approach to feedback fosters a culture of continuous learning and development within the organization.

Servant leaders recognize that valuable insights can come from all levels of the organizational hierarchy, not just those in senior positions. They create safe spaces for team members to share their thoughts, concerns, and suggestions without fear of reprisal. This inclusive feedback approach helps identify blind spots in leadership and uncover innovative ideas that might go unnoticed. Moreover, servant leaders model the importance of self-reflection and adaptability by consistently soliciting and acting upon feedback. They demonstrate that leadership is not about having all the answers but rather about being open to new perspectives and willing to adjust one's approach when necessary. This attitude of continuous improvement inspires team members to adopt similar mindsets, fostering a dynamic and resilient organizational culture.

Creating a culture where teammates feel empowered to provide honest feedback fosters an environment of trust, transparency, and collaboration. When team members feel comfortable sharing their perspectives and insights, they are more likely to communicate openly about issues, challenges, and opportunities for improvement. This open dialogue enhances problem-solving and decision-making and cultivates a culture of innovation and adaptability where new ideas and perspectives are welcomed and valued.

Practical strategies for soliciting feedback include incorporating simple questions into meetings or communication channels to gather input from team members. By ending meetings or emails with prompts such as "Do you have any feedback for me? Are there any things that I can improve on? What's working well for you?" servant leaders create opportunities for team members to share their thoughts and insights openly and honestly. This demonstrates a genuine interest in understanding the needs and perspectives of others and reinforces a culture of continuous improvement and mutual respect.

Furthermore, servant leaders actively listen to feedback with an open mind, seeking to understand the underlying concerns and perspectives behind the comments. They view feedback as a valuable source of insight and take proactive steps to address areas for improvement, demonstrating a commitment to personal and professional growth.

In essence, servant leaders recognize the importance of feedback as a catalyst for self-awareness, growth, and innovation. By fostering a culture where critique is welcomed, valued, and acted upon, servant leaders create an environment where individuals feel empowered to speak up, contribute ideas, and collaborate towards shared goals. Through their openness to feedback, servant leaders strengthen their leadership abilities and inspire and empower others to reach their full potential.

Here is a simple assessment tool to see your stand regarding servant leadership.

Self-Assessment: Principles of Servant Leadership

Reflect on each statement below and rate yourself on a scale of 1 to 5, where:

1 = Strongly disagree
2 = Disagree
3 = Neutral
4 = Agree
5 = Strongly Agree

1. I prioritize the needs of others above my own:
   ◦ Rating

2. I actively listen to understand the perspectives and concerns of others:

- Rating

3. I strive to empower and develop the people around me:

- Rating

4. I lead by example, demonstrating the values and behaviors I expect from others:

- Rating

5. I am committed to serving the greater good and advancing the collective goals of my team or organization:

- Rating

6. I am willing to make personal sacrifices for the well-being of others:

- Rating

LEADING BY SERVING ~ 69

7. I foster a culture of trust, openness, and collaboration:

- ○ Rating

8. I see leadership as a responsibility to serve and support others:

- ○ Rating

9. I acknowledge and value the contributions of every team member:

- ○ Rating

10. I am committed to continuous learning and self-improvement as a leader:

- ○ Rating

11. I actively seek feedback from others to better understand how I can support them:

- ○ Rating

12. I promote diversity, equity, and inclusion in all aspects of leadership:

- Rating:

13. I take responsibility for the well-being and growth of those under my leadership:

- Rating:

14. I am patient and understanding, especially during challenging situations:

- Rating:

15. I believe in the potential of others and work to help them realize it:

- Rating:

After rating yourself for each statement, reflect on areas where you feel strong and where you could improve. Consider actionable steps you can take to further embody the principles of servant leadership in your daily practice.[xii]

Chapter 10

Transformational vs Servant Leadership

Can you have both?

Servant leadership, at its core, is centered on prioritizing the needs and well-being of others above one's interests or comfort. While this often involves fostering positive relationships and uplifting team members, it also requires a willingness to make difficult decisions and provide constructive criticism when necessary, even if it may be unpopular or uncomfortable.

These leaders understand that avoiding tough decisions or shying away from giving negative feedback ultimately undermines their ability to serve their team effectively. By addressing issues head-on and providing honest feedback, leaders demonstrate integrity, accountability, and a genuine commitment to the growth and development of their team members.

Avoiding difficult decisions or withholding negative feedback may temporarily alleviate discomfort but ultimately erodes the team's trust, transparency, and respect. They recognize that genuine care and support sometimes require having difficult conversations and making tough calls for the greater good of the team and the organization.

Servant leaders foster a culture of accountability and continuous improvement within the team by embracing the responsibility of making unpopular decisions or delivering negative feedback. Rather than sugar-coating issues or sweeping them under the rug, leaders encourage open communication, honest dialogue, and a shared commitment to addressing challenges and driving positive change.

Practically, they approach unpopular decisions or negative feedback with empathy, compassion, and professionalism. They strive to communicate clearly and respectfully, acknowledging their decisions' impact while providing guidance and support to help team members navigate challenges and grow from the experience.

Ultimately, servant leadership is not about avoiding discomfort or seeking approval; it's about having the courage to do what suits the team, even when it may be difficult or unpopular. By focusing on their team members' long-term well-being and growth, servant leaders demonstrate integrity, authenticity, and a steadfast commitment to serving others, even in the face of adversity. Their actions inspire trust, build resilience, and empower individuals to overcome obstacles and achieve greatness together.

While servant leadership offers valuable principles for fostering a supportive and inclusive work environment, it is essential not to rely on it exclusively. Instead, incorporating it alongside complementary leadership styles like

Transformational Leadership can amplify its effectiveness and yield even more excellent results.

Transformational leaders take control of situations by conveying a clear vision of the group's goals. These leaders have a marked passion for the work and can make the rest of the group feel recharged and energized. Transformational leaders focus on helping group members support one another and provide them with the support, guidance, and inspiration they need to work hard, perform well, and stay loyal to the group. The primary goals of transformational leadership are to inspire growth, promote loyalty, and instill confidence in-group members.

Leadership expert and presidential biographer James MacGregor Burns introduced the concept of transformational leadership. According to Burns, transformational leadership occurs when "leaders and followers make each other advance to a higher level of moral and motivation."[xiii]

Bass also suggested that there were four different components of transformational leadership. The four main elements of transformational leadership are:

Intellectual stimulation: Transformational leaders are catalysts for change who challenge the existing status quo and actively foster and nurture creativity among their followers. These visionary leaders recognize the importance of innovation and continuous improvement in today's rapidly evolving business landscape. By encouraging their team members to think outside the box, transformational leaders create an environment that values fresh perspectives and novel approaches to problem-solving. These leaders understand that creativity is a robust tool for organizational growth and adaptation. They actively encourage their followers to explore new methodologies, techniques, and strategies for accomplishing tasks and achieving goals. This approach leads to more efficient and effective processes and empowers team members to take ownership of their work and contribute meaningfully to the organization's success.

Furthermore, transformational leaders strongly emphasize continuous learning and personal development. They actively promote new learning opportunities for their followers, recognizing that a well-educated and skilled workforce is essential for long-term success. These opportunities may include formal training programs, mentorship initiatives, cross-functional projects, or exposure to new challenges that stretch employees' capabilities and broaden their skill sets.

Individualized consideration: Transformational leadership extends beyond mere guidance, encompassing a vital aspect of nurturing and empowering individual team members. This leadership style strongly emphasizes cultivating supportive relationships within the organization. To achieve this, transformational leaders actively maintain open communication channels, creating an environment where followers feel comfortable and confident in expressing their ideas, opinions, and concerns.

This open dialogue serves multiple purposes. Firstly, it encourages innovation and creativity by allowing team members to voice their unique perspectives without fear of judgment. Secondly, it enables leaders to gain valuable insights into the thoughts and experiences of their followers, fostering a deeper understanding of their team's dynamics and potential. Moreover, transformational leaders are particularly adept at recognizing and acknowledging the distinct contributions of each team member. This immediate and personalized recognition goes beyond simple praise; it demonstrates a leader's attentiveness to individual efforts and reinforces the value of each person's role within the organization. By promptly acknowledging these contributions, leaders boost morale and inspire continued engagement and dedication from their followers.

Inspirational motivation: Transformational leaders can articulate a clear and compelling vision to their followers. These visionary individuals have a unique talent for communicating complex ideas in a way that inspires and motivates others. By painting a vivid picture of the future, they create a shared sense of purpose that resonates deeply with their team members. These exceptional leaders go beyond merely presenting a vision; they actively engage with their followers to help them internalize and experience the same level of passion and motivation that drives the leader.

Through their charismatic communication style and genuine enthusiasm, transformational leaders ignite a spark within their team members, fostering a collective commitment to achieving ambitious goals. By aligning individual aspirations with organizational objectives, these leaders create a synergistic environment where personal growth and collective success are intrinsically linked. This approach enhances team cohesion and cultivates a culture of continuous improvement and innovation as followers become emotionally invested in realizing the shared vision.

Idealized influence: The transformational leader serves as a powerful and influential role model for their followers, embodying the principles and values they wish to instill within their organization. This leadership style is characterized by the leader's ability to inspire and motivate through actions, words, and overall demeanor. Because followers have developed a deep sense of trust and respect for the leader, they are naturally inclined to emulate this individual's behavior and decision-making processes. This emulation goes beyond mere imitation; followers internalize the leader's ideals and core beliefs, integrating them into their personal and professional philosophies. This internalization process leads to a profound shift in the followers' mindset and approaches to their work, often resulting in increased commitment, creativity, and overall performance. The transformational leader's impact extends beyond day-to-day operations, fostering a culture of continuous growth, innovation, and shared vision within the organization.

Groups led by this type of leader tend to be successful and loyal. They give a lot to the team and care deeply about the group's ability to accomplish its goals. Turnover tends to be relatively low as transformational leaders can inspire great commitment in their followers.[xiv]

Transformational leaders possess a remarkable ability to inspire and motivate their followers to surpass conventional expectations. They accomplish this by skillfully shifting the focus from individual concerns to collective values and organizational needs. These leaders cultivate a sense of shared purpose and unity within their teams, fostering a collaborative environment where the group's success takes precedence over personal gain. Employees often develop a deep admiration for transformational leaders, drawn to their compelling vision for the future and their exemplary behavior that serves as a blueprint for others to emulate.

A cornerstone of transformational leadership is charisma, a magnetic quality that enables these leaders to connect with and influence their followers on an emotional level. This charismatic appeal is instrumental in rallying team members around a common goal and instilling a sense of enthusiasm and commitment. As a result, transformational leaders are frequently viewed as pivotal figures in driving organizational effectiveness, catalyzing change, and propelling their companies toward ambitious objectives.

In contrast, servant leaders adopt a distinctly different approach to leadership. Their primary focus lies in nurturing the growth and development of individual employees, helping them reach their full potential through personalized, one-on-one interactions. Servant leaders prioritize the needs of their team members, dedicating time and resources to support their professional and personal growth. A hallmark of this leadership style is the leader's tendency to attribute the team's successes to the efforts and achievements of their followers rather than claiming credit for themselves.

The question of which approach is superior is complex and context-dependent. Both transformational and servant leadership styles offer unique strengths and can be highly effective in different scenarios. However, an intriguing possibility emerges: can we synthesize the best elements of both theories to create a more comprehensive and adaptable leadership model?

A hybrid approach could potentially combine transformational leadership's inspirational vision and collective focus with servant leadership's employee-centric development and humility. This integrated style might inspire leaders to inspire grand organizational change while fostering individual growth and empowerment among team members. By balancing these complementary aspects, leaders could create a more resilient, motivated, and high-performing workforce capable of adapting to diverse challenges and opportunities in today's dynamic business landscape. By integrating Transformational Leadership with Servant Leadership principles, leaders can leverage the strengths of both styles to create a dynamic and high-performing team. Servant Leadership provides the foundation of trust, empathy, and collaboration to foster a supportive and inclusive work environment. At the same time, Transformational Leadership ignites passion, vision, and motivation to drive meaningful change and achieve ambitious goals.

By combining servant leadership's emphasis on serving others and fostering collaboration with transformational leadership's visionary and motivational aspects, leaders can create a synergistic leadership approach that maximizes their team's potential. This integrated approach enables leaders to inspire, motivate, and empower individuals to achieve extraordinary results, driving organizational success and creating a positive impact beyond the workplace.

While the theory of servant leadership resembles other leadership theories, none of the different theories encompass all the characteristics of a servant leader. A servant leader shares power, puts the needs of others first, helps individuals develop and optimize performance, is willing to learn from others, and forsakes personal advancement and rewards. Servant leaders concentrate on performance planning, day-to-day coaching, and helping people achieve. They provide vision, and their team understands their expectations and desired outcomes. The ultimate responsibility of the servant leader is the enduring investment of the leader's life in the lives of those who follow. As the ancient Chinese philosopher Lao Tzu said, "A leader is best when people barely know he exists; when his work is done, his aim fulfilled, they will say: we did it ourselves."[xv]

Chapter 11

Jesus as the Ultimate Servant Leader

Learning from The Teacher

Jesus was born into a world dominated by Greek and Roman culture, religion, and ideals. Their myths and stories were filled with gods who were petty, vengeful, lustful, and desperate to hold onto their power. Strength was the ultimate virtue; the strong could take what they wanted.

For instance, Chronos the Titan castrated his Father to take his power and become Earth's greatest deity and ruler. He then swallowed up his own children to prevent them from taking his place. It didn't work because Zeus would eventually defeat Chronos and take his place as the leader of the gods. Zeus tried to be a more benevolent leader, but he also had an insatiable lust for beautiful women and frequently acted upon it (which caused his wife, Hera, to take vengeance on these women).

In other words, this behavior was not just the stuff of myth and legends. The actual human leaders in this culture would have behaved the same way, and they would have celebrated behavior that demonstrated strength and power. Yes, sometimes that strength was used to enforce justice or maintain the "peace," but it was also motivated by personal glory and power.

The list could go on and on, but the ancient religions glorified gods for their power and strength, not for their kindness or love. In his Greek mythology book Mythos, Stephen Fry said that the "Greeks made gods in their own image, not the other way around."

Jesus Christ is often revered as the ultimate servant leader. In his interactions with others, He exemplified humility, compassion, and selflessness. Throughout his life and teachings, Jesus demonstrated a profound commitment to serving others, prioritizing their needs above his own, and offering guidance, support, and love to all who crossed his path.

Jesus demonstrated the qualities of a servant leader in the Bible—He cared for the least and the lost. He ate with them, engaged them, listened to them, and loved them. There are dozens of examples, but one of my favorite pictures of Jesus as a servant leader is the Samaritan woman at the well in John 4.

Jesus and the disciples were traveling through Samaria, and Jesus was tired. He decided to take a break at a well while the disciples went into town, but his timing was no coincidence. In The Bible exposition commentary, Warren Wiersbe points out that "He arrived at Jacob's well at six o'clock in the evening, the usual time for women to come for water." This means that Jesus was deliberately planning

LEADING BY SERVING ~ 81

to meet with this woman. He didn't summon her but went to her. And when she arrived, He spoke with her. He shared the gospel and led her to the well of living water.

There are several reasons it was unusual for Jesus to speak with the woman at the well:

She was a Samaritan – The text calls this out in verse 9 when it says, "For Jews do not associate with Samaritans." The Jews thought the Samaritans were scum and wanted nothing to do with them. But Jesus cared for her.

She was a woman – Again, the text calls this out in verse 27 when it says the disciples "were amazed that He had been speaking with a woman." It was not "proper" for a man to speak to a woman he did not know, but Jesus set aside social trends and customers to witness to a woman who needed truth.

She was a sinner. During their discussion, the woman admitted that she had no husband. In verse 18, Jesus says she has "had five husbands, and the one whom you now have is not your husband." Most people would have judged her harshly for this and avoided her at all costs, but not Jesus.

Most people looking to establish themselves as a great leader will seek out the powerful and the popular, but Jesus chose to seek out the people who needed him the most. Despite being a Samaritan woman and a sinner, Jesus cared for the woman at the well, took the time to engage with her, and pointed her to the Truth. She was saved and shared the good news with her whole town.

Today, we must remember the least and the lost. The best leaders focus on helping those who need it most, enabling them to grow, change, and become contributing team members. They listen to people who seem less important and make everyone feel valued. As the woman at the well demonstrated, when people feel valued, they are far more likely to follow you and join in your mission.[xvi]

Social or cultural boundaries did not limit Jesus' healing ministry. He reached out to people from all walks of life, including the poor, the outcasts, and even those considered unclean or undesirable by society. His willingness to engage with those on the margins of society challenged social norms and highlighted his commitment to inclusivity, justice, and compassion for all.

Another iconic example of Jesus' servant leadership is depicted in the biblical account of the Last Supper. In a powerful display of humility, Jesus washed his disciples' feet, a task typically reserved for servants. By performing this act of service, Jesus demonstrated the importance of humility and selflessness in leadership, teaching his disciples to serve one another with love and humility.

Moreover, Jesus' ministry was characterized by compassion and empathy towards the marginalized, the oppressed, and the outcasts of society. He reached out to the sick, the poor, and the sinners, offering them healing, forgiveness, and hope. In doing so, Jesus modeled a servant leadership style that prioritized the needs of the most vulnerable and marginalized members of society, demonstrating a profound commitment to social justice and inclusivity.

Jesus also exemplified servant leadership through his willingness to sacrifice himself for the greater good. His ultimate act of service was his crucifixion, where he willingly laid down his life for the redemption and salvation of humanity. In this act of selflessness, Jesus embodied the essence of servant leadership, showing that authentic leadership involves sacrifice, love, and a willingness to serve others at all costs.

LEADING BY SERVING ~ 83

> *But among you it will be different. Whoever wants to be a leader among you must be your servant,* [27] *and whoever wants to be first among you must become your slave.* [28] *For even the Son of Man came not to be served but to serve others and to give his life as a ransom for many."* Matthew 20:26-28

Jesus' teachings profoundly emphasized the transformative power of love, forgiveness, and compassion as cornerstones of effective leadership. He consistently urged his followers to embody these virtues, encouraging them to love one another with the same depth and sincerity he demonstrated. This radical approach to interpersonal relationships extended beyond mere sentiment, advocating for tangible expressions of kindness, empathy, and respect in all interactions.

Central to Jesus' leadership philosophy was the revolutionary concept of servant leadership. He challenged the prevailing notions of authority and power by elevating humility, meekness, and a servant's heart as essential qualities for those in positions of influence. This paradigm shift encouraged leaders to prioritize the needs of others above their own, fostering a community-oriented approach to guidance and decision-making. By emphasizing these virtues, Jesus presented a leadership model that was both compassionate and transformative, capable of inspiring profound change in individuals and communities alike. His teachings resonate across cultures and centuries, offering timeless wisdom for those seeking to lead with genuine care and selflessness.

Jesus taught the importance of sacrificial love as the defining characteristic of true discipleship. He taught his followers to love one another as he loved them, laying down their lives for one another (John 15:13). This selfless love, rooted in the example of Jesus' sacrificial death and resurrection, serves as the foundation of servant leadership, inspiring individuals to prioritize the needs of others above their own and to serve with humility, compassion, and grace.

His sacrificial love exemplifies the essence of servant leadership, demonstrating the profound impact that selfless love and sacrifice can have on individuals and communities. His death on the cross and resurrection offers a powerful reminder of the transformative power of love, redemption, and forgiveness, inspiring countless individuals to follow his example and serve others with unwavering devotion and compassion.

Jesus' healing ministry is a powerful example of servant leadership, illustrating his bottomless compassion, empathy, and commitment to serving the needs of others, especially the most vulnerable in society. His actions remind us of the transformative power of compassion and the importance of reaching out to those suffering, marginalized, or oppressed, embodying the essence of servant leadership in its purest form.

Teaching and mentoring are fundamental components of servant leadership, and Jesus' role as a teacher and mentor was pivotal to his ministry. This role exemplified His unwavering commitment and genuine desire to empower others, enabling them to realize their full potential and divine purpose. Throughout His earthly sojourn, Jesus invested considerable time and effort in fostering the growth and development of His disciples, guiding them with profound wisdom, infinite patience, and boundless compassion.

A notable aspect of Jesus' teaching and mentoring approach was His willingness to engage with His disciples on a profoundly personal level. He consistently allocated time to listen to their myriad questions attentively, pressing concerns, and lingering doubts, demonstrating genuine care and heartfelt empathy for their struggles and collective challenges. Whether elucidating complex parables, clarifying intricate theological concepts, or addressing their deepest fears and insecurities, Jesus patiently walked alongside His disciples, providing the tailored guidance and unwavering support they required to deepen their understanding of spiritual truths and strengthen their faith.

Jesus' mentorship extended beyond mere instruction, encompassing a holistic personal and spiritual growth approach. He led by example, demonstrating the virtues and principles He taught through His actions and interactions. This experiential learning allowed His disciples to witness firsthand the practical application of His teachings in various real-life situations. Moreover, Jesus created a nurturing environment that encouraged open dialogue, critical thinking, and personal reflection, fostering a dynamic learning experience that transcended traditional teacher-student relationships of the time.

Jesus' role as a teacher and mentor exemplifies servant leadership in its purest form. Through his patient guidance, compassionate care, and empowering leadership, Jesus invested in the growth and development of his disciples, equipping them to carry on his mission and make a lasting impact on the world. His example challenges us to embrace the call to serve others with humility, compassion, and love, following in the footsteps of the ultimate servant leader.

Jesus used various teaching methods to effectively communicate his message and impart wisdom to his disciples. He employed parables, analogies, and real-life examples to illustrate spiritual truths and principles, making his teachings accessible and relatable to his audience. Through his engaging and thought-provoking teaching style, Jesus fostered an environment of active learning and reflection, encouraging his disciples to wrestle with profound truths and apply them to their lives.

Additionally, Jesus demonstrated servant leadership by leading by example in his interactions with his disciples. He modeled humility, integrity, and selflessness in everything he did, inspiring his followers to emulate his character and values. Through his actions and words, Jesus taught his disciples what to believe and how to live, inviting them to walk in his footsteps and embody the principles of the Kingdom of God. Jesus' approach to leadership was revolutionary for his time, emphasizing service over authority and compassion over power. He consistently put the needs of others before his own, as exemplified in washing his disciples' feet—a task typically reserved for servants. This powerful demonstration of humility challenged conventional notions of leadership and hierarchy.

Jesus' integrity was evident in the alignment between his teachings and his actions. He lived out his preached values, showing unwavering commitment to truth, justice, and love. This consistency in character earned him the trust and devotion of his followers, who witnessed firsthand the transformative power of his example. By inviting his disciples to emulate his way of life, Jesus created a model of discipleship that transcended mere intellectual agreement. He encouraged active participation in the Kingdom of God,

LEADING BY SERVING ~ 87

where believers were called to manifest divine love, forgiveness, and righteousness daily.

This holistic approach to faith and leadership continues influencing Christian thought and practice, inspiring believers to lead lives of purpose, compassion, and selfless service. Jesus gave his disciples the tools and resources to spread his message. He entrusted them with authority and responsibility, empowering them to perform miracles, heal the sick, and proclaim the good news of salvation. By empowering his disciples to carry on his work, Jesus demonstrated his confidence in their abilities and his commitment to empowering others to make a difference in the world.

We cannot overlook Jesus' sacrificial love as the pinnacle of servant leadership, demonstrating unparalleled selflessness, compassion, and dedication to serving others. His willingness to lay down his life for the redemption of humanity is the ultimate example of servant leadership, inspiring countless individuals to follow and embody the same sacrificial love in their lives.

At the heart of Jesus' sacrificial love was his profound commitment to fulfilling the will of his Heavenly Father and bringing salvation to humanity. Despite facing unimaginable suffering and agony, Jesus willingly endured the cross, bearing the weight of humanity's sins and offering himself as the ultimate sacrifice for the forgiveness of sins. His death on the cross was not merely a random act of violence but a deliberate and purposeful demonstration of love, compassion, and redemption.

His sacrificial love was characterized by his willingness to endure humiliation, rejection, and betrayal for the sake of others. Throughout his ministry, Jesus faced opposition, persecution, and betrayal by one of his disciples. Yet, in the face of adversity, Jesus responded with love and forgiveness, extending grace and mercy to those who wronged him.

These examples illustrate how Jesus Christ embodied the principles of servant leadership throughout his life and ministry, inspiring countless individuals to follow his example and serve others with humility, compassion, and love.

Chapter 12

Why be a Servant?

What are the benefits of Servant Leadership?

Servant leadership represents a transformative approach to leadership, one that not only empowers individuals but also enriches the organizational culture. At its core, servant leadership prioritizes the needs and development of others above all else. This philosophy extends far beyond the traditional hierarchical leadership model, instead fostering a collaborative environment where everyone is valued and supported in their growth journey.

Servant leadership fosters a strong team culture by empowering team members and instilling a sense of ownership and accountability. Unlike traditional leadership models, where directives flow from the top down, servant leaders distribute responsibility and decision-making authority among team members, encouraging them to take ownership of their work and contribute meaningfully to the team's overall success. This approach cultivates a collaborative and supportive environment where team members feel valued, motivated, and deeply invested in the team's goals and objectives.

Servant leaders empower their team members by granting them the autonomy to make decisions and take initiative in their work. Rather than micromanaging or meticulously controlling every aspect of the team's activities, servant leaders trust their team members to exercise their judgment and expertise to accomplish tasks and solve problems effectively. This sense of autonomy increases team members' motivation and engagement and encourages them to think creatively and innovatively, leading to improved performance and outcomes.

Furthermore, servant leaders create abundant opportunities for team members to develop and grow professionally by providing challenging assignments, facilitating skill-building and development initiatives, and offering constructive feedback and unwavering support. By investing in their team members' growth and development, servant leaders demonstrate their steadfast commitment to personal and professional success, fostering a culture of continuous learning and improvement. This investment in human capital pays dividends through increased loyalty, enhanced skills, and a more adaptable workforce.

Servant leaders also foster a culture of collaboration and teamwork by promoting open communication, mutual respect, and trust among team members. This creates a safe and inclusive space for dialogue, feedback, and idea-sharing, encouraging team members to collaborate seamlessly and support one another in achieving common goals. By prioritizing transparency and inclusivity, servant leaders ensure that every team member's voice is heard and valued, creating a profound sense of belonging and camaraderie within the group. This leadership approach extends beyond immediate team dynamics, influencing the broader organizational culture. By modeling servant leadership behaviors, these leaders inspire others to adopt similar practices, creating a ripple effect throughout the organization. This can improve cross-functional collaboration, employee satisfaction, and a positive work environment.

Servant leaders are adept at recognizing and leveraging the unique strengths of each team member. They take the time to understand individual capabilities, interests, and aspirations and then align these with team objectives. This personalized approach optimizes team performance and increases job satisfaction and employee retention. One of the most profound benefits of servant leadership is its ability to strengthen team dynamics. By serving the team rather than commanding it, leaders inspire trust and respect among team members. This trust forms the foundation of effective collaboration, enabling teams to work cohesively towards shared goals. As a result, productivity flourishes, minimizing conflicts and creating a harmonious and supportive work environment.

This type of leadership cultivates a vibrant culture of inclusivity and openness, where every voice, regardless of position or background, is heard and genuinely valued. Leaders who wholeheartedly embrace this approach go beyond passive acceptance of ideas; they actively and enthusiastically seek input from their team members at all levels of the organization. These leaders recognize and appreciate that diverse perspectives, shaped by varied experiences and expertise, are the cornerstone of superior decision-making processes and groundbreaking innovation.

The inclusive culture fostered by this leadership style does more than encourage creativity; it nurtures an environment where novel ideas can flourish and evolve. Team members feel empowered to share unconventional thoughts without fear of judgment, leading to a rich tapestry of concepts and solutions. This atmosphere of psychological safety and mutual respect instills a profound sense of belonging and ownership among employees, transcending mere job satisfaction. As team members see their contributions valued and implemented, their emotional investment in the organization deepens. This heightened level of engagement further strengthens their commitment to the organization's mission and long-term goals. The result is a workforce that is not just aligned with the company's objectives but is passionately dedicated to driving the organization forward, creating a powerful synergy between individual aspirations and collective success.

Another significant advantage of servant leadership is its focus on personal and professional development. Servant leaders invest in the growth of their team members, providing mentorship, coaching, and opportunities for learning and skill development. Servant leaders cultivate a sense of purpose and fulfillment among employees by aligning individual aspirations with organizational objectives. This alignment enhances employee engagement and drives organizational performance, as individuals are motivated to contribute their best efforts towards shared success.

Servant leadership is a powerful catalyst for fostering resilience and adaptability within organizations. By prioritizing the well-being of their team members, leaders create a supportive and nurturing environment where individuals feel valued, respected, and empowered. This approach cultivates a sense of psychological safety, encouraging employees to take calculated risks, voice innovative ideas, and embrace change without fear of repercussion. In such an atmosphere, team members are more likely to develop a growth mindset, viewing challenges as opportunities for learning and development rather than insurmountable obstacles.

This mindset shift is crucial in building organizational resilience, enabling employees to bounce back from setbacks and adapt to new circumstances more quickly and confidently. The adaptability fostered by servant leadership is vital in today's fast-paced and unpredictable business landscape. Organizations must be agile and responsive to remain competitive with technological advancements, shifting market dynamics, and global events that are continually reshaping industries.

By empowering their teams and promoting a culture of continuous learning and improvement, servant leaders equip their organizations with the tools necessary to navigate these complex challenges effectively. This leadership style encourages open communication and collaboration, allowing for the rapid dissemination of information and the cross-pollination of ideas. Such an environment is conducive to innovation and creative problem-solving, essential for organizations seeking to evolve and stay ahead in their respective fields. By nurturing adaptability at all levels of the organization, servant leaders ensure that their companies are well-positioned to seize new opportunities and overcome obstacles in an ever-changing business world.

Servant leadership is not just a leadership style but a philosophy permeating every aspect of an organization. By placing people at the center of leadership, servant leaders create a culture of trust, collaboration, and growth, laying the groundwork for long-term success and sustainability. As organizations continue to navigate complex challenges and opportunities, embracing the principles of servant leadership will be essential in building resilient, high-performing teams and fostering cultures of excellence and innovation.

Thomas A. Mayberry is a seasoned leadership expert and author with over forty years of experience. Passionate about servant leadership, he has dedicated his career to helping leaders develop the skills and mindset necessary to foster environments of trust, collaboration, and sustained growth. He is a speaker and workshop facilitator known for his engaging and inspiring presentations. His commitment to empowering leaders extends to his writing, where he shares his knowledge and experience. Author of five previous books, Thomas witnesses how his Christian faith has impacted his personal and professional career.

To learn more about Thomas, please visit his website, https://thomasamayberry.com

His previous works include:

Faith Guided Leadership: What defines your style?

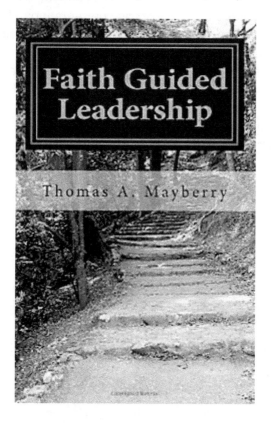

What defines your leadership style? Are you reaching your potential as a leader? How would your leadership style change if you had God in the center of your life? If you let Him guide you toward being a more effective leader, how much of a difference would it make? The qualities of a strong leader are given to us in the Bible. God has shown us the path to fulfilling our potential. Do we ignore Him and fall prey to the ways of the world or do we follow His teachings and positively influence all of the people that we associate with? The choice is yours. This book is written from the perspective of a manager who was trying to fit into corporate America. Tom took on the same traits as the people that he reported to. He felt that the way to succeed was to learn from those who had succeeded before him. It took 20 years and almost two marriages for him to learn where to put his priorities. Once he refocused his life on God, it showed through in his style of leadership. Today, he stays true to his faith in God and does not worry about what others think is the only way to lead a team. He knows the one true way.

Stress Free Living: Is it possible or just a dream?

Is your goal to become stress-free? Is it really possible? Can you live your life without any stress? We live in a world surrounded by stressful situations. Some of these situations we have control over and we can dictate how much stress we allow. In other situations, we do not have control over what happens. In this case, we still need to control how much we allow it to increase our stress level.

Some say that it is not possible to live without stress. The main purpose of this book is to help you acknowledge and manage your stress. You should be able to control the stress factors in your life so that they do not control you. I repeat that you may not be able to control what happens in all situations. You can, however, be aware of your stress level and maintain control over it. You need to be able to tell the signs of stress so that you can react and relax.

I have been asked by many of my friends how I picked stress management as the topic for my second book. I primarily have focused my attention on how to lead people. Stress management has an impact on the way that you lead people more than you think. It is crucial to create a stress-free work environment to be able to get more out of your team. I enjoy watching sports. I see many athletes who can stay calm in pressure situations and lead their teams to victory.

This same approach can be applied to all aspects of your life that you are a leader. I have been blessed with the ability to stay calm and relaxed in most situations. I will share some of the techniques with you throughout this book. If it came down to just using techniques, we would all live stress-free. You need to approach stress management with the right attitude. I apply a Christian approach, as I do in most areas of my life. This has made a huge impact on my life.

Use this book as a tool. Refer back to it regularly when you need extra support in situations. This book will not change your life overnight. It is a journey that we are taking. This book will help you along in your journey to take control of your stress and to be a better leader.

A very personal book about valuable lessons in dealing with stress.

A Marathon Journey: Lessons in Goal Setting

    A Marathon Journey is an inspirational look at how you can achieve your goals, no matter how daunting they may seem. It is told through the point of view of a man in his fifties who pursued running as a way to lose weight. The author had never run more than a mile at a time in his life, but within eighteen months, he was able to run three half marathons and a full marathon. Thomas breaks down goal setting into manageable steps to enable you to achieve even your most elusive goals.

40 Days of Reflection: Devotions for Lent

Lent is a time of repentance and acknowledging where we have fallen short of God's expectations. We set aside these 40 days to reflect on our relationship with God. How can we build a closer, stronger relationship? Some people "fast" or give up things that are dear to them for Lent. Consider how you can grow during this time. Think of this as a self-assessment, but instead of for your employer's annual review, it is a time to look at yourself through God's eyes. Are you doing the things God wants you to do? Are you exhibiting the traits of Jesus?

Faithful Steps: Developing a closer relationship with God

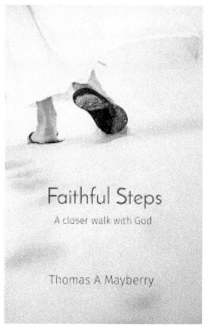

In a world filled with constant distractions and the hustle and bustle of everyday life, we find ourselves longing for something more. As we navigate the challenges and complexities of our existence, we realize that a void within our souls must be filled. As you turn the pages of this book, you will be inspired to look within, embrace your spirituality, and embark on a transformative journey toward a profound connection with God. It reminds you that no matter where you are on your path, you can always take steps toward deepening your relationship and experiencing the boundless love and guidance that awaits.

i https://en.wikipedia.org/wiki/Robert_K._Greenleaf

ii The Servant Leader, Ken Blanchard and Phil Hodges, Copyright 2003 page 24

iii https://www.biblegateway.com/passage/?search=Matthew%2014:13-21&version=NIV

iv https://www.cnbc.com/2019/07/16/third-of-us-workers-considered-quitting-their-job-in-last-3-months.html

v https://ccc.bc.edu/content/ccc/blog-home/2024/01/mentoring-in-workplace-examples-best-practices.html

vi https://situational.com/blog/five-reasons-why-trust-matters-at-work/

vii https://www.linkedin.com/pulse/ripple-effect-positive-leadership-transforming-customer-april-sabral-f733e/

viii https://leaders.com/articles/leadership/servant-leadership/

ix https://nimblequotes.com/alone-we-can-do-so-little-together-we-can-do-so-much-helen-keller/

x https://www.indeed.com/career-advice/career-development/how-to-be-a-leader

xi https://ccaps.umn.edu/story/10-steps-be-better-leader-your-community

xii https://chatgpt.com/c/ed41d8cb-e0b3-4493-acb5-44268ec8f9bd

xiii Allen GP, Moore WM, Moser LR, Neill KK, Sambamoorthi U, Bell HS. The role of servant leadership and transformational leadership in academic pharmacy. Am J Pharm Educ. 2016;80(7):113. doi:10.5688/ajpe807113

xiv https://www.verywellmind.com/what-is-transformational-leadership-2795313#citation-1

xv https://www.brainyquote.com/quotes/lao_tzu_121709

xvi https://app.logos.com/books/LLS%3A29.3.5